SHALL THE MURDERER GO UNPUNISHED!

The Life of Edward H. Rulloff
New York's Criminal Genius

SHALL THE MURDERER GO UNPUNISHED!

The Life of Edward H. Rulloff
New York's Criminal Genius

STEPHEN D. BUTZ

North Country Books
Utica, New York

Shall the Murderer Go Unpunished!
Copyright © 2007
Stephen D. Butz

ISBN-10 1-59531-015-0
ISBN-13 978-1-59531-015-6

Library of Congress Cataloging-in-Publication Data

Butz, Stephen D.
  Shall the murderer go unpunished! : the life of Edward H. Rulloff,
New York's criminal genius / by Stephen D. Butz.
     p. cm.
  Includes bibliographical references.
  ISBN 978-1-59531-015-6 (alk. paper)
  1. Rulloff, Edward H. (Edward Howard), 1819-1871. 2. Murderers--
New York (State)--Binghamton--Biography. 3. Murder--New York
(State)--Binghamton. I. Title.
  HV6248.R8B88 2007
  364.152'3092--dc22
  [B]
                                          2007009866

Book design by Zach Steffen & Rob Igoe, Jr.

Cover map courtesy of www.historicaltownmaps.com

North Country Books, Inc.
311 Turner Street
Utica, New York 13501
www.northcountrybooks.com

CONTENTS

FOREWORD

What does it mean when a man's brain has been preserved for antiquity? Who on this earth gains such importance as to have a piece of his body saved forever? These were the questions that I sought to answer when I began to research the life of Edward H. Rulloff. As a graduate student at Cornell University, I first learned of Rulloff when I discovered his unusually large brain which lay in a jar on display in Uris Hall on campus. Most of the other brains in the Wilder Brain Collection were those of great thinkers from the nineteenth century, except for Rulloff's, and I began to wonder who this man was. The story that unfolded as I delved into his life was fascinating, so much so that it almost felt as if I were piecing together a work of fiction.

The timeline of Rulloff's life is extraordinary to say the least. He first gained prominence in Ithaca, New York, during the 1840s as a brilliant young physician and school teacher, who also had an interest in the formation of human language. However, this promising future came to an abrupt end in 1845 when he was accused of the disappearance and murder of his young wife and infant daughter. This began a series of incidents that led to one of the most exciting criminal investigations and legal battles of nineteenth century America. The events that occurred after the disappearance of Rulloff's family involved a spectacular cross-state manhunt, a jail break, mob violence, and brilliant legal wrangling by none other than Rulloff himself. Incredibly, all during this tumultuous time, he managed to continue his work formulating a theory on the formation of human language and nearly established himself as a respected scholar.

As time went on, Rulloff shifted his operations to New York City, where he headed a crime syndicate that spread its tentacles into many illegal pursuits. All the while, he led a double life as an intellectual who was making a name for himself in the circle of elite linguists of 1860s New York. Eventually, after years of supporting his research by leading a life of crime, Rulloff met his end in the hangman's noose, shocking many of his fellow scholars, who knew nothing of his dark side. After his execution he became known as the man with two lives, the devil scholar, the monstrum horrendum, the leader of the "Trinity of Crime," and the great criminal and philologist. Edward Rulloff's story is the tale of a frustrated scholar who turned to crime to support his pursuit of knowledge, often in reckless abandon and with an apparent lack of morality. For him everything was secondary to his quest to complete his thesis on language.

In writing this biography I have attempted to interpret and re-breathe life into someone who made his mark on society long ago and in such a unique manner. This is indeed a challenge, as author Richard Norton Smith described best when he wrote, "For who among us possesses the omniscience [or humility] to authoritatively interpret the character and motivations of another human being." To meet this task, I have tried to use the words of those who knew Rulloff when he was alive and to recount events as accurately as possible. Luckily, Rulloff's own thoughts still live on in the many letters he wrote throughout his life which survive to this day.

TO BE A GENTLEMAN

Edward H. Rulloff was born Edward Howard Rulofson on the third of March, 1819. His parents' home was located in the small village of Hampton, just outside the city of St. John, in the province of New Brunswick, Canada. Edward's father, William, was one of six children raised by Rulof Rulofson, a British loyalist who had served as an ensign in the New Jersey Volunteers during the American Revolution. William married Priscilla Howard in 1818, and the two were soon raising Edward and his two younger brothers. The three Rulofson brothers were all destined for greatness, although the methods they used to achieve it were not at all similar. Because of their children's natural intellect and desire to succeed, it must be assumed that the Rulofson parents possessed exceptional character. As an adult, Edward Rulloff said he owed much of his education to his mother, for his father had died when he was five or six years old. After their father's death, the Rulofson boys' mother was aided in their upbringing by one of their uncles.

Not much else is known about the early childhood of Edward H. Rulofson (hereafter referred to as Rulloff), but it has been passed down through the lore of the city of St. John that he possessed an exceptional intelligence as a boy. Some stories tell that he mastered the ancient languages of Greek and Latin at the age of five and went on to learn algebra and trigonometry at age seven. It will never be known if Rulloff actually achieved these feats of intellect that early, but it is apparent that he possessed an incredible memory and had a never ending interest for reading at an early age. His devotion to the study of languages also began to be nurtured when he was young, as he stated later in life that "...[I] had never been in a college or university, but from boyhood had a most intense interest in the beauty and strength of the Greek tongue."

Rulloff often spoke of how his mother helped to nourish his love of knowledge. As a boy, he spent the majority of his days in the pursuit of learning. He soon became the talk of his small town as the boy prodigy, who would amaze the locals with his intellect. People who knew Rulloff during this time described him as a young man with a marvelous memory and magnetic personality with which he impressed not only average citizens but learned men as well.

After his father's death, Rulloff became more immersed in reading and less concerned with the world around him. His mother would often have to remove the candles from his room at night in order to stop him from reading and coax him to go to sleep.

Rulloff began his formal schooling by entering into the St. John Academy in New Brunswick. While there, he continued to nurture his interest in the study of languages by studying ancient Greek and Latin along with French, German, and Spanish. At the age of fourteen he abruptly left the academy at the insistence of his uncle to find a profession. This suggests that the death of Rulloff's father may have put a financial strain on the family. It may also be possible that the boy believed he had learned all that could be taught to him at the school, therefore prompting him to move on in search of higher learning.

Rulloff later recalled these formative years, "[My] father died when [I] was five years old, and an uncle took care of [me]. [I] went through school and got through the high schools, studying all the English branches before [I] was fourteen. [My] uncle declined to have me study the classics unless [I] was to enter a profession. [I desired] to study them and be a gentleman. [I] wished to lay a broad foundation and acquire a general education."

After leaving the academy, Rulloff took on a job as a clerk in the law office of Duncan Robertson, a noted barrister in the city of St. John. His job at the law office allowed him to continue to learn as well as earn money, as he later recollected, "[I] entered into a lawyer's office as clerk, simply for the purpose of earning a living, and at the same time to have leisure to pursue [my] studies." At the law office, he most certainly gained a wealth of legal knowledge which he would put to use later in life. However, while employed by the barrister his learning was not limited to the study of law, but also involved chemistry and botany.

Rulloff's drive to educate himself was unique during the 1830s, as it was certainly rare for a fourteen-year-old boy to pursue such a self-taught curriculum. This alone points to Rulloff's unique disposition and exceptional intelligence. He spent his time so diligently in the pursuit of knowledge that he often forgot to eat. Rulloff stayed with the law firm for two years, eventually leaving to find work as a clerk in a local store. Why he moved on from the firm is unknown, but he may have felt that he had absorbed all he could about the law. Whatever the reason, Rulloff's new vocation at the store also came with its fringe benefits, as he later revealed, "keeping [my] books open on the counter, and taking every leisure moment for study."

Rulloff's passion for learning seemed to take precedence over everything else in his life, which must have been a constant struggle for him. He also felt pressure from his uncle to pursue a trade and begin an apprenticeship. During the early 1800s, a general education was difficult to come by and was mostly reserved for those of wealth. While the teenage Rulloff was struggling to educate himself, he lost his mother. Although the cause of her untimely death is unknown, it certainly would have been difficult for the Rulofson boys to loose both parents in such a short span of time. The death of their mother may have been the reason all three of them eventually left St. John. Ruloff Rulofson, who was the middle child, eventually established a successful sawmill in western Pennsylvania, which made him very wealthy. The youngest of the three brothers, William Rulofson, traveled to California and became a successful photographer.

At the time that Rulloff was employed as a clerk, he was approximately seventeen years old. While Rulloff worked at the store it caught fire twice and much of the structure was damaged. Strangely, the remains of the merchandise that was housed in the portion of the building that was consumed by fire were never recovered. Rulloff eventually left his job under suspicion from his employer that he was the cause of the fires and responsible for the disappearance of the clothing.

The last job he held in his hometown was that of an apprentice in an apothecary, which must have satisfied both his need to learn and his uncle's insistence that he find a trade. His time spent learning the art of pharmacology was cut short, however. This was due to a series of strange incidents that began to reveal Rulloff's dark side, along with the emergence of his egotistical mannerisms.

One day young Rulloff was approached by his former employer, the owner of the dry goods store that had twice been mysteriously burned. The store owner confronted him and accused his former clerk of arson and thievery. The store owner explained that if Rulloff confessed to the crimes nothing more would be said of it and no legal trouble would be brought against him. Maybe he felt sorry for the bright young man who had recently lost his mother and hoped the confrontation would put him back on the path of rightness. However, Rulloff shocked the store owner by angrily exclaiming that he, "May do as [he] pleases with this matter!"

A few days later, Rulloff was once again confronted in the street by his former employer. This time, however, Rulloff was wearing a suit of clothes that had been reported lost in one of the fires. Whether it be the result of his inflated ego or a case of absentmindedness, Rulloff was caught with the stolen goods, arrested, and tried for theft. All hope for a promising future for the town prodigy seemed lost, and he was sentenced to two years in the penitentiary at St. John.

The prominent nineteenth century lawyer S.D. Halliday later wrote about this dark period in Rulloff's life, "The saddest scene that ever occurs in court is when some young boy for some first offense is sent to prison for the first time. I have no faith in so-called reformatories. I think there should be written over the door of every prison, whatever may be its name, the words that were written by Dante over his terrible *Inferno*: "Abandon all hope, ye who enter here.""

After serving his sentence, Rulloff was released from prison in 1839. He was now twenty years old and, like his brothers, left his home in New Brunswick never to return again.

OF FINE APPEARANCE AND FASCINATING ADDRESS

fter Rulloff's release from prison he traveled to New York City. His time spent in jail must have been a harsh reality, for his pursuit of knowledge was most assuredly put to a halt during his internment. His motivation for heading towards New York was most likely the result of his need to distance himself as far from his homeland as possible, for he had almost certainly lost all of the respect he ever had there. Also, New York was one of the largest cities on the east coast. What better a place to establish a new life and catch up on his lost scholarship? This growing city held libraries that would indeed be of interest to a man of learning.

Rulloff's vision of arriving in America, where he could begin a new and better life, matched that of all the immigrants who were arriving in New York at that time. However, as many found out, New York City in the 1840s could be a harsh place to eke out a living. The only account of Rulloff's life during this period was written by E.H. Freeman, one of Rulloff's earlier biographers: "In New York City Edward met a Mr. Gourand, a teacher of a commercial school who promised, after he had become more proficient in bookkeeping, penmanship, [etc.], to guaranty [*sic*] him a situation; Rulloff found Mr. Gourand [to be] a humbug and a fraud, who took his money as long as he had any, and failed to comply with his agreement."

It is interesting to note that the twenty-year-old Rulloff ended up working at a school while in New York. He must have used his considerable knowledge to gain a job with the school, but he left shortly after he was hired. With no money or personal contacts, he was a lost soul in the fast-paced port city. Realizing that New York was too much for one so used to the quiet life of rural New Brunswick, he left in search of work elsewhere. His efforts to leave New York paid off when Rulloff met up with Captain William Hedger, who was running a boat on the Erie Canal between Ithaca, New York, and New York City.

Stretching for more than 250 miles, the Erie Canal linked New York to the Great Lakes region via Albany, Syracuse, Rochester, and Buffalo. The canal was part of the changing face of the growing United States. Because of this grand waterway and smaller ones like it, a new economy began to emerge in the country. Now it was possible for western farmers to ship their crops to growing East Coast markets. As a result of the opening of the canal, the average freight charge to ship goods from Buffalo, New York, to New York City dropped from approximately nineteen cents per ton per mile in 1817, to two cents per ton per mile in 1830.

Rulloff found himself in the middle of this boon in trade as he tried to establish a new life in 1840. Captain Hedger's meeting with Rulloff was recalled by Amelia Krum, whose grandfather was a relative of Hedger's, "[Hedger] was running boats to New York, and on one of his return trips, after disposing of his load, [was] walking one day on the tow path to see that the boats were all right. He met a young man who seemed in distress, and he with his usual kindness inquired the trouble. Rulloff, whom it was, claimed he had been robbed and was destitute, and wanted to get a place to work, he would do anything, so Mr. Hedger offered [a] place with him as he was short of help, and he [Rulloff] gladly accepted the place [position] to drive the mules on the tow path for him."

It was to Captain Hedger that the former Edward H. Rulofson introduced himself for the first time as Edward Rulloff, the name he used almost exclusively for the rest of his life. This was either an attempt by Rulloff to change his persona to hide from his past as the petty thief he became in St. John, or just a simplification of his European name, which was quite common during the period. So it was that Rulloff became part of the history of the Erie Canal. His life on the canal was short-lived, however, for it lasted only as long as the trip from New York City to Ithaca.

The arrival of Captain Hedger's canal boat in the small city of Ithaca brought more change into Rulloff's life. Ithaca lay nestled at the southern end of Cayuga Lake, the second largest of the Finger Lakes of Central New York. Cayuga Lake stretches thirty-nine miles north to the city of

Seneca Falls, and it is there that the Erie Canal joins with the lake. Hedger's home was located just east of Ithaca in the small village of Dryden. Once they docked, Rulloff was asked by Hedger's relative, William Schutt, who also worked on the canal boat, to join him at his home in Dryden. This invitation was later recalled by Amelia Krum, "[Rulloff] proved himself a capable workman and an interesting and intelligent young man; so upon their arrival at Ithaca, Mr. Schutt invited him to accompany him to his home."

Dryden, New York, at the time of Rulloff's arrival, was a booming lumber town. The region possessed a great quantity of high-quality pine trees, and although Dryden was only a small village, it housed fifty-three lumber mills. The area was also blessed with an abundance of flowing water which was used to power the mills. Lumber became the principle means of employment and commerce in the village of Dryden during the middle part of the nineteenth century. Many debts were paid in wood to local merchants by those who lacked other means to pay their bills or purchase goods.

Rulloff moved into William Schutt's farmhouse, where he was received warmly by the simple country folk. His advanced intellect was quite apparent to the hardworking Schutt family, who made their living by working the land. At first he adjusted to the hard life afforded to farmers, but he soon grew restless and anxious to once again pursue his scholarly interests.

It didn't take long for Rulloff to reconnect to the life that he once had while growing up in St. John. Shortly after arriving in Dryden, he ventured into Ithaca in search of a better means of employment. What he found there was the opportunity to become a clerk in a local drug store. His previous employment in pharmacology certainly must have helped him gain a position there. It was also during this time that he returned to formal schooling. Rulloff began to attend the Ithaca Academy where he resumed his studies of the Greek language. The only other student in his class of classical Greek at the time was Francis M. Finch, who would later become Rulloff's lawyer, lyric biographer, and legal savior. It appears that Rulloff received special attention at the Ithaca Academy, for he would only attend once a day to recite in Greek. This arrangement allowed for him to also begin a serious study of botanical medicine with a local herb doctor by the name of Day. Rulloff recalled these seemingly promising days, "[I] commenced the study of medicine with the intention of becoming a physician, but also continued [my] study of languages."

During this period in his life, things began to look up for Rulloff. He had left his past behind and was creating a new life for himself in Ithaca with hope for a successful future. His reputation for being a man of learning must have caught the attention of many of his fellow citizens, for early in 1842 he began to teach penmanship at night in the nearby village of Slaterville. Rulloff was an exceptional penman, as can be seen in the many letters which he wrote that still exist today. He is said to have taught so many pupils during this time that he eventually left his job as clerk at the pharmacy to become a full-time teacher.

Because of his growing popularity, Rulloff had been asked by the townspeople of Dryden to open a select school there, and in late 1842 he became a private school teacher. The school building in which he taught was located on Main Street. Further evidence to support Rulloff's fine reputation in the area at the time is expressed by a description of him as a teacher by Mrs. Krum: "All the young men and young ladies who were anxious to secure a better education than was afforded them at the district school, attended his school...Rulloff was fine-appearing, and of fascinating address; and being finely educated, was a favorite among those who considered him above the average country youth."

It is interesting to observe that Rulloff was regarded as "finely educated," since he was predominantly a self-taught man and was only twenty-three years old. Most of the vast knowledge he possessed was the result of his own determination to "lay a broad foundation [in] a general education...and be a gentleman." The people in the Ithaca area must have been quite impressed with this man who had just recently arrived from New York City. It would seem that Rulloff was successful in establishing a new life and leaving behind his sordid past; however, it didn't take long for the dark side of his character to emerge once again.

Two events occurred during Rulloff's tenure as Dryden's school teacher which revealed his true nature, as recounted once again by Amelia Krum. The first event involved one of his students: "[Rulloff] said something abusive to one of the young men, who was his pupil...thereby causing a deep feeling of resentment, and it was decided by two of the young men that [Rulloff] should receive some chastisement and they resolved to give him a 'good whipping' when he came from his school. But Rulloff learning in some way of their intentions, remained securely locked in the school room, not daring to venture forth for many hours, until the young men had grown tired of waiting for him. Later the affair was reconsidered and terminated without trouble."

The other incident involved a confrontation with a citizen of Dryden village concerning the actions of some of Rulloff's students: "[Mr. Tyron] reproached the young men for making unnecessary noises in the church while they were holding services. Rulloff resented the remark and speaking to [Tyron] in French in an abusive manner...Rulloff struck him with his cane. This caused some excitement among those who saw it done and a bitter feeling was aroused against [Rulloff]. But the next day [Rulloff] sent a letter of apology to [Tyron], regretting his hasty act, and the matter was dropped."

These two actions, occurring within a short span of time in Dryden, began to further reveal Rulloff's true nature. In both incidents his abusive manner seems to come forth before his rational reasoning. This uncontrollable temper and extreme self-centered attitude formed the hallmarks of Rulloff's personality, which would steer him into trouble that would plague him the rest of his life. These two incidences were also significant in their similarity to the way that Rulloff conducted himself while in St. John. Even in his new life in Dryden, where he was highly regarded, he maintained a self-centered attitude towards the world around him. It appears that two years in prison did not change him.

While he was teaching at the select school in Dryden, another significant event began to unfold in Rulloff's life. One of his students was the younger sister of William Schutt, with whom Rulloff resided upon first arriving in Dryden. Harriet Schutt was a young girl of sixteen or seventeen who was said to have natural beauty. Her relationship with Rulloff was described by writer Edward Crapsey, who observed, "Almost from the beginning of the school his attentions to Miss Schutt were those of a lover, and were accepted by her as such. In age, the parties were not unequally matched, and in mental acquirements as well as worldly prospects, he seemed far her superior."

Crapsey's observations of Rulloff's love interest were presented in his book, *The Man of Two Lives*, published in 1871. Although at many times overly dramatic, his book provides a reasonable account of some of Rulloff's exploits. Even Rulloff's onetime brother-in-law, Ephriam Schutt, assured that Crapsey's accounts about the time were "truthful as far as it goes." It is interesting to note that before becoming an author, Edward Crapsey was a newspaper correspondent for the *Philadelphia Inquirer*, covering the American Civil War. In one instance during the war, Crapsey was accused of slander by Union General George Meade, who subsequently had Crapsey ridden out of his camp sitting backwards on a mule while wearing a sign which read "Libeler of the Press." Crapsey's incident caused most Northeastern papers to exclude mention of General Meade, unless of course he was involved in defeat.

The relationship between Harriet Schutt and Rulloff resulted in their marriage on the 31st day of December 1843, nearly one year after his arrival in Ithaca. Crapsey recalls this event as one much discouraged by the entire Schutt family, even to the point where William Schutt, Harriet's brother, demanded that Rulloff present some proof of his previous life prior to coming to Ithaca before proceeding with the wedding. This seems unlikely considering it was William Schutt who had been so impressed with Rulloff when they worked together on the Erie Canal that he brought him home to live with his family.

It has also been claimed by Crapsey that, "The Schutt family instinctively shuddered as they saw this paragon insidiously creeping into their domestic circle...in spite of the protests of her family, who, regardless for their fondness for him, seemed to have a premonition of trouble and also felt that too little was known of his past." This is also doubtful, as Rulloff was apparently highly regarded in the Dryden community, unless the Schutt family's opinion of him was changing as his true personality began to reveal itself. These apparent contradictions about how Harriet's family viewed Rulloff are most likely the result of Crapsey's flair for the dramatic.

The following description made by another Rulloff historian is probably a more accurate characterization of Rulloff at the time of his marriage: "He was a botanical physician, a druggist, an excellent penman, a classical scholar, a mechanist of rare original power, a lawyer, and an earnest, fluent speaker. There was apparently nothing he could not do, or attempt, and being moreover possessed of good address and polished manners, to the unlettered rustics [of Dryden] he seemed a marvel..."

The year 1844 began with the young Rulloff couple starting out their new life together. However, the marriage would also cause the emergence of Rulloff's jealousy, a flaw that, when coupled with his selfishness and quick temper, would prove disastrous.

A WATERY GRAVE

*A*t first the newly married couple lived in the Schutt family home, and Rulloff soon left his teaching position at the Dryden school to begin practice as a botanical physician. It was also during this time that Rulloff become obsessed with one of his wife's cousins, Dr. W. H. Bull. It was only a couple of weeks after their wedding that an incident occurred which would lead to a series of troublesome events between the two. Dr. Bull often visited the Schutt home, and on this one particular occasion he kissed all of the Schutt women in greeting, including the new Mrs. Rulloff. This act outraged Rulloff to the point that he left the house and walked off in a rage.

Jealousy was not the only thing that separated Bull and Rulloff, for they also held different views on how best to practice medicine. Rulloff sided with the botanical method, which utilized the many natural compounds that existed in trees and herbs, as a means to treat his patients. This method required that physicians have a vast knowledge of the effects of natural compounds and how they would work in conjunction with one another. Botanical medicine was the precursor to today's modern science of pharmacology.

Dr. Bull used another approach to medical treatment, which at the time was called the "old school" of medicine, also known as Allopathy. Allopathic medicine followed the doctrine of treating disease by producing a condition which is antagonistic to the ailment to be cured or alleviated. Often, the new ailment would be more harmful to the patient than the original disease. Needless to say, the medical division which existed between Bull and Rulloff must have created great tension and occasional arguments whenever the two met, an antagonism made worse by Bull's seemingly overly affectionate attention to the women of the Schutt family. Many men and women have felt the power which jealousy can have over them, and within Rulloff, who already possessed a short temper and strong self-ishness, this feeling was uncontrollable.

Dr. Bull increasingly became a point of discontent between Rulloff and his wife. On another occasion he again stormed out of the Schutt house in a rage over Dr. Bull. Shortly afterward, Rulloff spoke to his brother-in-law, William Schutt, about the incident. He told him that such affections were completely out of line, and if he were one of the women being approached by Bull, he would certainly kill him. That night he left his wife at her family's home and rode into Ithaca with William, who later recalled their conversation: "He had left his wife once or twice; he said he disliked Dr. Bull and couldn't bear to have him near his wife; Bull was his wife's cousin; this was their first meeting after the marriage...he said he didn't think his wife had any intercourse with Dr. Bull, but he hated him; at another time he said (that same evening) pretty much the same thing as before; he then said he thought Dr. Bull and his wife had had intercourse together; said he thought he should leave her..."

During this time Rulloff stopped teaching school and devoted all of his time to the practice of medicine. As a doctor, he successfully gained the confidence of a large portion of the community, and he became known as a highly respected botanical physician. His friendship with his wife's brother William was also at a high point at this time. Luckily, William resided in Ithaca and did not become involved in the strife that was developing as a result of Dr. Bull, although William's older brother, Ephriam, did, as he later recalled, "There was some difficulty between them, but I never wit-nessed any; I once heard her crying in a room; went into the room; they were all together; I asked him (Rulloff) why he treated his wife so; he made no particular reply; I said to him his conduct was very strange, and asked him if he could not conduct himself in a different manner, and if his wife was not agreeable, to leave her to us, but otherwise stay; he finally concluded to stay; this was in the winter following their marriage."

Eventually the trouble that was brewing between Rulloff and Dr. Bull led to violence. Dr. Bull had come to the Schutt house to borrow a wheel-barrow. Upon Bull's arrival, Rulloff left the house without saying a word.

He was gone all night, probably in Ithaca at the office of Dr. Stone, another physician with whom Rulloff had studied medicine. Upon his return the next day, he found his wife and her sister Jane in the family kitchen. Mrs. Rulloff was pounding peppercorns with a pestle. Rulloff complained that she was not pounding them fine enough for his liking, whereupon he tried to snatch away the pestle to show her how to do it correctly. When she refused, he grabbed the pestle and struck her with it on her forehead. Jane Schutt later recalled the incident, " [I] don't think that the pepper was a playful matter; didn't hear any angry words at the time; can't say what he said except that the pepper wasn't pounded fine enough; he drew the pestle from her and struck her; it was a marble pestle; I think it was a hard blow; it knocked her back several steps; he made some apologies; he said he didn't intend to strike her so hard; he appeared shocked and surprised that he hit her so hard; she insisted that he did it on purpose…"

This event caused the Schutt family to look at Rulloff in a much different way. Rulloff attributed his attitude towards his wife to Dr. Bull's attentions to her. At one time prior to this act of abuse, Rulloff had overheard a conversation that took place between his wife and Dr. Bull in a nearby mill. Rulloff claimed that he heard Bull say to his wife that she was being seduced by him and might be again soon. Harriet Rulloff allegedly turned the approach off with a laugh and did not appear to resent the remark. This must have fueled the fire that was burning inside of Rulloff, for once he arrived at the family farmhouse he began to pack up his things, intent on leaving his wife. During this frantic moment, Rulloff took up his wife's wedding dress and told her that "he wouldn't leave it with her, for in three weeks she would have it on and be with Dr. Bull." He stormed out of the house leaving everything behind except the dress.

Upon his return, the elder Schutt turned him away from the house, which Rulloff didn't set foot in again for many months. However, a few days after the wedding dress incident, his wife joined him at Jan O'Brien's boarding house in Ithaca, where he had been staying. His wife hoped that moving away from her family's house would leave the trouble Rulloff was having with Dr. Bull behind. This was unfortunately not the case, for before long Rulloff's irrational behavior and jealousy once again turned to trouble for the young couple.

Harriet's brother, William, was a merchant in Ithaca and resided in a house on the south hill which overlooked the town. He continued to have a good relationship with the couple during their stay at Jan O'Brien's boarding house. When he had to go away on business, William asked if the Rulloffs would oversee Harriet's younger sister, Mary, who was living with him. One evening while at dinner in the boarding house, Rulloff became incensed over his brother-in-law being away for too long. He demanded that the younger sister of his wife walk home to the family farm house in Dryden. His wife protested, saying that her sister was only eleven years old, and the distance was over nine miles. The couple then left the dinner table and went upstairs to their room, leaving the young girl downstairs alone.

The event that followed was described by one of the other guests staying at the boarding house at the time: "I heard a noise [upstairs and] went up; Mrs. Rulloff stood by the foot of the bed with a pillow before her mouth, and he had a vial in his hand; he said that [damned] bitch was going to poison herself; he was not near her; she said, 'Oh, Edward, [aren't] you ashamed of yourself?'...I [then] went downstairs and started to go."

The commotion continued, and soon Mrs. O'Brien ran upstairs to see what was wrong:

> "I went up and saw her, and she said, 'Oh Jane, come up quick!' Mrs. Rulloff said, 'Edward is going to make me take poison and take it himself;' they were clinched together; he had the bottle in his hand, and [Mrs. Rulloff and I] tried to take it away; I took hold of her; he said, 'By the living God, this poison will kill both of us in five minutes,' and that would put an end to their troubles; he saw [we] were getting the better of him, and he threw it out of the window; then they got over the excitement, he began to twit her about Bull, and she dropped on her knees and said, 'Oh, Edward, I am innocent as an unborn child;' he struck her in the face, and said, 'Get away God damned you; you know better than to come near me when I am angry as I am now;' the blow knocked her over; she looked very red in the face; he told her she could go and live with Dr. Bull, and seek all of the pleasure she wished to, for he didn't want to live with her anymore; he charged her with sexual improprieties; his language was pretty broad...I advised him to go away and leave her; Rulloff said that before he would leave her to another he would serve her as Clark did his wife; Clark murdered his wife."

After this violent incident, Rulloff and his wife left the boarding house with the young Mary Schutt and returned to Dryden. Three days later Rulloff once again showed up at the boarding house; this time he held a letter in his hand that was apparently from William Schutt, who was still away on business. Rulloff was definitely agitated at what was written in the letter, for he told Mrs. O'Brien that he sometimes felt like destroying the entire Schutt family.

Rulloff's rage was not just directed at the Schutts, however, for a few days later the Rulloffs were invited to a party attended by many local families. Upon their arrival, a minister greeted Mrs. Rulloff by kissing her. Rulloff told his brother-in-law that he did not believe in that type of greeting, and if he was a woman he would murder a minister before he would permit him to kiss her. Rulloff was so enraged by the gesture that he left with his wife, exclaiming that he would never take her anywhere again.

A few days later, Dr. Bull boldly came to visit them in Ithaca. Bull's motives are unclear, but he must have been aware of the animosity that Rulloff held toward him. Upon Bull's arrival, Rulloff stormed out of the house, leaving his wife behind weeping. A short time later, the couple moved into their own house in the village of Lansing, New York. Lansing was located approximately five miles north of Ithaca, in the midst of beautiful rising farmland located near the eastern shore of Cayuga Lake. The couple arrived in their new home in the fall of 1844, where they lived as peacefully as they ever had. Rulloff's medical practice kept him quite busy during this period, and in April Mrs. Rulloff gave birth to a baby daughter, whom they named Mary.

While Rulloff resided in Lansing, he was summoned to the home of his brother-in-law William, whose wife had taken ill. She too had recently given birth, but had never fully recovered after the delivery of her baby. Rulloff attended to her, but her condition declined. Soon the newborn baby also fell ill, and Rulloff suggested that his mother-in-law, Hannah Schutt, be summoned to watch over them. While riding in a carriage towards Ithaca from her Dryden Home, Hannah Schutt had an odd conversation with Rulloff which she later recalled: "Rulloff wanted me to go and take care of her [William's wife]; said he supposed I felt anxious for her to get well; then Rulloff said that William had misused him about Dr. Bull, and that thing would yet mount up to the shedding of blood; on the way to William's he said it was strange that I had raised so many children without losing any, but my gray hairs would yet go down in sorrow to the grave; he said William's wife and child [are going]; who will go next? He said Harriet and her babe would go next." William's wife and newborn daughter died shortly thereafter, only a few days apart of one another.

While residing in Lansing, Rulloff began to focus his attention away from his medical practice and to the development of an original theory on the formation of language. He expressed to his friends that "since an early age [I] became impressed with the idea that [I] had a high destiny to fulfill in the development of a lingual theory which would greatly simplify the study of language." Rulloff believed that the ancient Greek language held the key to this discovery, and it was in the study of this language that Rulloff began to immerse himself. His home in Lansing was rather small, but in it he began to put together quite an impressive library. It was also during this time that Rulloff's brother Ruloff Rulofson moved from Central New York to Pennsylvania, a short distance from the Finger Lakes region. The significance of his brother being nearby at the time is important for events to come.

Ruloff Rulofson left St. John when he was twenty-one years old to begin a life as a millwright. During this period of time, lumber was being sought as a means to build the great cities which were growing rapidly all along the east coast of the United States. North America possessed some of the finest timberland in the world. The old growth forests of the northeast were composed of trees like chestnut, hemlock, pine, and spruce that would rival the size of today's western redwoods. The lumber business was becoming very profitable for the extremely hardworking men who could harvest and mill these trees.

Ruloff Rulofson was one such man. In 1843 he constructed the first successful live gang sawmill in the United States. A gang saw is a group of saw blades that make multiple cuts into a log simultaneously, producing lumber at a much higher rate, thus greatly improving the efficiency of a sawmill. Because of the nature of the lumber business at that time, which was to completely clear-cut entire tracts of forest, he eventually decided to move his lumber operations down into Elk County, Pennsylvania, which was only one hundred fifty miles southwest of Ithaca. Western Pennsylvania, Ohio, and Indiana were booming, as farmers from the rocky hills of New York and New England began to move west in search of more arable farmland. This was the western frontier at the time, where land was readily available and fortunes were waiting to be made.

Although it may never be known for certain if Rulloff was in contact with his brother during this period, it is very likely that he was. The two were very close when they were growing up, and much later in life, Rulloff kept in contact with him. His brother's move into Pennsylvania may have caused Rulloff to express interest in moving west, where he could possibly find a position with a college where he could teach and continue to develop his theory of language formation. His wife's intentions were clear, however; she did not want to move too far away from her family in Dryden. It will never be known if this was the cause of more trouble between them.

One evening in June of 1845, Rulloff and his wife were returning home with their infant daughter after visiting Harriet's parents. Rulloff stopped the carriage in which they were driving and spoke to his wife, "Harriet, I want you to get up in the wagon and look over the old place for you will never see it again."

Harriet rose up in the wagon holding her child and gazed out at her family's farm; she told her husband that it was a beautiful sight to behold. She returned to her seat and the Rulloff family rode off. A few days after this incident, Harriet related the account to her sister, who was visiting them in Lansing. Whether Rulloff's statement was a threat or a reference to his decision to move his family westward is unknown, but it foreshadowed a most horrid event.

On June 24, 1845, Harriet Schutt crossed the road from her home in Lansing, holding her child in her arms, to borrow some soap from her neighbors, the Robertsons. Elizabeth Robertson gave Harriet the soap, and she returned to her home. Later that same day, Rulloff showed up at the Robertson's door to ask if someone might be able to go over and stay with his wife while he ran some errands in town. He was concerned about the presence of a group of Native Americans in the vicinity of Lansing, and he said that if his wife were alone she would be frightened. Mrs. Robertson's daughter, Olive, went to stay with Mrs. Rulloff until her husband returned.

Olive Robertson's later testimony described what occurred that evening, "I was at home that night; Rulloff was at our house; he told me to go to his house, that his wife might be afraid if she knew that Indians were there; I stayed until nine o'clock and went home. Mrs. Rulloff was holding her child in her lap when I went away...[Rulloff] came with the Indians with him; [the] Indians stayed a short time; while they were there [Rulloff] showed Mrs. Rulloff and myself the jewelry and moccasins the

Indians had with them; [Rulloff] then gave the Indians something, I thought it was money; after the Indians left, I think I saw him stirring something in a tea-cup; [I] think he said it was composition tea...[I] never saw Mrs. Rulloff or child since." Olive Robertson was the last person to see Mrs. Rulloff and her daughter alive.

The next morning around ten or eleven o'clock, Rulloff arrived at the Robertsons' door once again. He asked if he could borrow a horse and wagon, with which he would deliver a chest of his wife's uncle's belongings. Mr. Robertson agreed and instructed his son, Newton, to harness the horse and bring it around to Mr. Rulloff's house. A short time later, Robertson looked out of his window to see his son and Rulloff struggling with a large wooden chest. Robertson approached the two and asked if they needed help. Rulloff replied that he would be very pleased if he would, and the three men then lifted the chest into the wagon. Later, Robertson would claim that the chest was very heavy and that his end probably weighed sixty or seventy pounds.

Robertson also inquired about the whereabouts of Rulloff's wife. Rulloff told him that she had gone off with her uncle to the village of Mottville, New York (today known as Brooktondale), which was about ten miles southeast of Lansing. Rulloff then drove off in the wagon heading south on the road toward Ithaca. After his departure, Robertson noticed that all of the shutters on Rulloff's house were closed tightly, which was not the usual case. Rulloff was not seen until the next day, when he returned with the wagon and the chest.

What exactly occurred on the night of June 24, or early the next morning, has been speculated on by lawyers, writers, and historians for over one hundred years. Although the accounts vary, one thing is certain: Edward H. Rulloff murdered his young wife during that time. Whether it was premeditated or the result of his violent temper will never be known, but because of his previous actions of spousal abuse, as recollected by those who witnessed them, it seems likely the death of his wife may have been the result of his uncontrollable rage and not something that was planned. Whatever the cause of this violent crime, Rulloff certainly felt no remorse after it had been done, or if he did feel remorse, he hid it very well. The fate of his infant daughter, Mary, is shrouded with even more mystery.

The Robertson's son saw Rulloff return home the next day with the same chest that he had helped load into the wagon. Rulloff lifted the chest out by himself, and to the Robertson boy it appeared much lighter than before. Mr. Robertson went over to retrieve his wagon and noticed that the horse had not been driven too strenuously, for the past few days had been very hot, and the horse did not show signs of fatigue. Rulloff took lunch with the Robertsons, and then later in the afternoon was seen walking south on the road towards Ithaca. Mrs. Robertson recalled that Rulloff was carrying his wife's shawl over his shoulder and appeared to be carrying something inside of it.

That same evening he was seen in Ithaca at the home of his sister-in-law, Jane Schutt. Rulloff arrived at her house looking very worn out. He asked her if she had anything to eat, which she did not, so he went into her cellar and ate whatever bread and vegetables he could find. Rulloff told Jane that his wife was at home, and he was planning to take his family to a place between Seneca and Cayuga Lakes. While he was there, he also offered to take some baby clothes home with him. After leaving Jane's, Rulloff went to the home of William Schutt, where he took tea. He sat down to read a passage from the book, *The Mysteries of Paris*, and began to openly weep. He told William that he could never read that passage without crying. Later, Rulloff removed a ring from his pocket and showed it to William. He asked him if he recognized it. William said that he did, because it was the same ring he had given to his sister Harriet many years before. Rulloff then asked him if he would like it back. William replied that he would not, and that it should be returned to his sister. After this strange encounter, Rulloff left William's house and was seen removing some of his belongings that he had kept at Dr. Stone's office. Afterwards he disappeared from the area.

The exact whereabouts of Edward Rulloff for a period of about six weeks after June 25 are not known, but there are several theories regarding where he might have been. The most intriguing of these is that he was staying with his brother Ruloff Rulofson in Elk County, Pennsylvania, and that he may have visited his newly wedded brother for the purpose of finding a home for his infant daughter. This seems entirely plausible, especially if Rulloff's temper, as many believe, was the cause of his wife's death. If this was true, then what was the fate of his daughter Mary? Could he have been cold hearted enough to kill her as well?

Sources who were close to Rulloff when he was in Binghamton twenty-five years later said they knew what took place in Rulloff's home in Lansing on the night of June 24. One of these, a lawyer by the name of Charles Ford who was a friend of Rulloff's, made a deathbed confession to one of the Schutt family relatives. The dying Ford summoned Landon Krum, who was a cousin of Mrs. Rulloff, to his bedside. Mr. Ford told Krum that, "The body of Mrs. Rulloff lies on the bottom of Cayuga Lake near the Taughannock Falls ravine where the water in the lake is the deepest. Weighted with heavy irons to prevent it from ever being seen again, it was sunk by her husband...After being murdered in her home by her husband, Mrs. Rulloff was placed in a chest, and carried to the watery grave."

Although there were many people who claimed to know the facts of this crime, the account given by Mr. Ford is probably closest to the truth. Unlike other people connected to the case, Mr. Ford did not attempt to make money from his knowledge of Mrs. Rulloff's fate. In fact, he kept it a secret until his final days. Also, his account supports very closely what the circumstantial evidence suggested. Rulloff was known to have a bad temper and he quarreled frequently with his wife. He was also observed to have become physically violent with her on at least two occasions prior to her disappearance. It is plausible that on the night of June 24, Rulloff might have been quarreling with his wife about moving out west or about her relationship with Dr. Bull, which may have resulted in him striking her in some manner, causing her death. If this is true, then her murder was the result of rage and not premeditated, for if it had been premeditated, he would have surely covered his tracks much better than he had. This, however, still leaves the mystery of what happened to his daughter.

After killing his wife, Rulloff would have realized that he must dispose of the body in order to hide his heinous crime and evade conviction. Strong circumstantial evidence suggests that his wife was indeed in the chest that the Robertsons helped load into their wagon. Upon leaving the house, Rulloff had most likely already chosen the lake as the best place to get rid of her body. Portions of the east side of Cayuga Lake near Lansing are very steep, and the depth of the lake increases rapidly from the shore. The area is also fairly remote, making it the perfect place to sink something in order to conceal it forever. Both William and Jane Schutt, who saw him the day after the disappearance of his wife, noticed that his face was very sunburned. This could have been the result of traveling along the shoreline in search of the perfect location to deposit his wife's body into the lake. Also, the east side of the lake near Lansing is located approximately five miles south of the region where Mr. Ford said Rulloff sank the body of his wife, near the Taughannock Falls ravine. This puts the location within easy traveling distance from Rulloff's home.

Another interesting revelation made by Mr. Ford in his deathbed disclosure was a mention of the fate of the infant Mary Rulloff. Mr. Ford relates that Rulloff did not murder his daughter, but gave her to an unknown family to be raised as their own. Furthermore, the girl was alleged to have grown up in Pennsylvania and to have eventually married. Coincidently, Rulloff's younger brother, who resided in nearby Pennsylvania, raised a daughter named Priscilla Jane Rulofson who was very close in age to that of Rulloff's own daughter. Could Priscilla actually be Rulloff's missing child? Critics of this theory would point out that the infant was not anywhere to be seen during the time that Rulloff was disposing of his wife and visiting Ithaca. Certainly a two-month-old child could not have been left unattended in Rulloff's Lansing home without the neighbor's knowledge, for they certainly would have heard it crying.

It may be that after Rulloff murdered his wife, he sought help from the two Native American women who had been in his house earlier that evening. The part they play in this mystery will never be known, but Rulloff's interactions with them suggest that he was on good terms with the women. Maybe his daughter was left in their care until he was able to leave town. The baby clothes Rulloff took from his sister-in-law's house the day after he killed his wife seem to add credibility to this theory. Although based only on circumstantial evidence and a deathbed confession, this theory certainly is plausible.

The only aspect of this theory that causes some difficulty is the eyewitness account of the stagecoach agent who was working at the Clinton House office in Ithaca on the night of June 26. He witnessed Edward Rulloff boarding the stage going north to Geneva, New York. Rulloff signed the stage register with the name John Doe and took with him two chests. One carried his belongings from Dr. Stone's office; the other contained items from his Lansing home. Rulloff definitely boarded the stage without his daughter. Could it be that Rulloff arranged to pick her up on his way to Geneva, then dropped her off with his brother to be raised as his own? Or did he simply leave her with the Native American women? The other dreadful conclusion about the fate of his daughter, of course, was that he murdered her as well. None of this may ever be known unless the remains of his victims are recovered.

Evidence of Rulloff's whereabouts after June 26, 1845, surprisingly shows up in Chicago, Illinois, in the form of a promissory note that he signed. Apparently he borrowed twenty-five dollars from a real estate agent there by the name of Richard Swift. The note was dated August 4, 1845, and was signed in Rulloff's own hand. He left one of the chests he was carrying when he boarded the stage coach in Ithaca with Swift as security for his loan. Why he traveled to Chicago, or what he did for the entire month of July is unknown. One thing is clear, though: he never returned for the chest he left as collateral for his loan, and it was opened later by Swift, who recorded that it contained "...a large bundle of papers, lectures on phrenology, Hooper's Dictionary, E. H. Rulloff written on the inside cover... names of persons; small box containing women's fixings; papers in bottom of box; letters; cards marked Edward H. Rulloff; a paper on which were the words, 'Oh that dreadful hour!' one lock of light brown hair in paper, labeled a lock of Harriet's...lace cap for an infant...small sea shells."

The paper that was found in the chest, on which was written "Oh that dreadful hour!" is also revealing. Was this line referring to the night he killed his wife, and why would he have written just that one line and left it in his chest? Was he in the process of admitting his guilt? Or maybe it had something to do with explaining his circumstances to his brother who may have taken charge of his child.

About two or three weeks after Rulloff and his wife were last seen together by the members of the Schutt family, two of Harriet's brothers went to visit them in Lansing. When they arrived they found that the Rulloffs were not at home. They inquired of their whereabouts at the Robertsons', who told them that the Rulloffs had gone away between the lakes. At that time the Schutts didn't try to enter the Rulloff house; however, later that same day a man by the name of Dr. John Burdick showed up at the house looking for some books that he had loaned Rulloff. Upon hearing that the Rulloffs were to be away for awhile, he went to the owner of the house, a man by the name of Fields, and inquired if he might borrow a key which would allow him to enter the house so he could retrieve his books. Fields agreed to let him in, and the two men returned to the house together and opened the door. Upon their entry, Dr. Burdick described what they found, "Fields and I went in; I didn't find my books...saw some dirty clothes in the washroom; saw a skirt at the foot of the bed laying in a circle; also stockings, shoes, elastics; some dishes on the table, unwashed..."

The general disarray of the Rulloff home, described by Dr. Burdick, suggested that Mrs. Rulloff was not visiting between the lakes. The fact that most of her belongings were still in the house pointed to foul play. After this event, rumors began to circulate around Ithaca that Mrs. Rulloff and her child may have been murdered. A few weeks later a large group of concerned citizens, lead by Sheriff Porter of Ithaca, gathered at the Rulloff home. The Schutt brothers were also present as the sheriff entered the Rulloff house and found it exactly as previously described. Ephriam Schutt, however, made another important observation, "I visited [Rulloff's] house when suspicions were raised; I know [Rulloff] had a cast iron mortar that would weigh twenty-five or thirty pounds; he had flat irons; on search could not find anything of them…"

The missing mortar and flat irons may have been used to weigh down Harriet's body so it sank deep into the lake, although the significance of this observation wouldn't be realized until much later. As the group began to disperse from the Lansing home, murder must have been on all of their minds.

AND YET A MURDERER!

*I*n August of 1845, William Schutt and his brother Ephriam were present at Hale's store, which was owned by William. It was late in the day, and the two brothers were relaxing and speaking of the day's events, when surprisingly, Edward Rulloff walked through the front door. It had been nearly two months since anyone had seen either of the Rulloffs, and both of the brothers jumped to their feet and greeted him with much excitement. William immediately asked where he had been, and Rulloff replied that he was staying between the lakes, near Geneva. He was then asked if his wife was there, to which he replied yes. William took Rulloff upstairs to a private room and asked him if he knew that the townspeople believed he had murdered his wife and child. Rulloff appeared to be surprised by the remark and said that he could not believe that anyone would think such a thing. Rulloff then inquired if it was safe for him to be out in the street. William told him that the sheriff might detain him until he could prove that his wife was still alive. Later that day Rulloff changed his explanation of his wife's whereabouts. He now said that she was in Pennsylvania, near the town of Erie. Schutt commented that he was surprised that Rulloff had convinced his sister to travel so far from home, since she always wanted to be near her family.

That night Rulloff appeared restless, and when asked what was wrong, he replied that it troubled him to think the people of Ithaca believed he was a murderer. The next day a few men confronted Rulloff and demanded to know the exact whereabouts of his wife. He began to appear nervous and asked his brother-in-law Ephriam what he should do. Ephriam replied that he should immediately write her a letter and remain in Ithaca until she replied. Rulloff began to compose a letter, which he ripped up shortly after he started writing. He then wrote a second letter, which he completed. Strangely, this letter was addressed to someone by the name of N. Depuy, who lived in Madison, Ohio. The men who had gathered to confront Rulloff were given the letter and asked to mail it.

Although Rulloff's life is filled with many strange circumstances, his return to Ithaca after a six week disappearance is probably the most perplexing. His motivation for coming back to the city is difficult to determine. What is equally bizarre is how the whereabouts of his wife changed three times in one day, from Geneva, to Erie, Pennsylvania, and finally to Madison, Ohio! For such an intelligent man, he certainly didn't think too much about how to account for his wife. Probably the best observation made of this strange move was given by S.D. Halliday during a lecture about Rulloff's life on December 28, 1900: "It is a well understood fact that there is a kind of indescribable fascination to a criminal about the place where he has committed a crime, and however far he may go away, still he wants to come back...Such seemed to have been the impelling influence that compelled Rulloff to return from Chicago to Tompkins County...He unblushingly, and without trepidation...visited his wife's brothers and sister."

Shortly after the group of men who demanded proof that his wife was alive left Rulloff to go mail the letter, he seized the opportunity and quickly departed Ithaca on foot towards the town of Auburn. He must have finally realized the precarious situation he had put himself in and thought it best to flee. Later that same day, a man who had been watering his horse a few miles out of town was passed by a man making his way rapidly north. When this man arrived in Ithaca a few hours later, he found the town being turned upside down in search of Edward Rulloff. He immediately told the sheriff about the person he had seen heading north so quickly. The sheriff put Ephriam Schutt in charge of the manhunt, and Schutt immediately headed off in the direction of Geneva to try and cut off Rulloff's escape.

When Schutt arrived in Geneva he boarded the next train and searched it, but found no signs of Rulloff. He then decided to continue on to Rochester. Once there, Schutt patiently waited for each train to arrive and subsequently searched them. His decision to travel to Rochester paid off when he eventually located Rulloff, who had been hiding on the rear platform of a car filled with immigrants who were headed west. With his knowledge of languages, Rulloff could have easily mixed in with a group of recent arrivals from Europe. Once confronted, he surrendered himself peacefully to his brother-in-law, and the two continued to ride the train to Buffalo.

When they arrived, the two weary travelers checked into a hotel. Ephriam wisely secured one room for the two to sleep in and kept a watchful eye on his brother-in-law throughout the night. The overnight stay at the hotel in Buffalo must have been difficult for both of the men. There is no record of the words exchanged between the two during this time, but Rulloff most assuredly must have claimed that he was innocent and that his wife and child were still alive. One must admire Ephriam Schutt for single-handedly taking on the job of apprehending his brother-in-law. Rulloff was known to have a tendency for violence and was by no means a small man, as described in a wanted poster produced by the sheriff to aid in his identification and capture: "Said Rulloff is about 5 feet 8 inches high, stout built, short thick neck, large head, man of quick precise motions, and stoops forward when he walks, speaks English, German, and other languages, and has a beard...weighs 180 pounds, measures round the chest 40 inches, round the waist 37 or 38 inches, broad between the eyes, dark brown hair, rather small dark blue or hazel eyes, broad full face..."

The next morning in Buffalo, Schutt decided to give Rulloff the benefit of the doubt, and he purchased two tickets for travel on board a boat headed for Fairport Harbor, Ohio. Rulloff must have convinced his brother-in-law that the whole thing was a great misunderstanding and that his wife and daughter were alive and staying in Ohio. Schutt brought Rulloff down to the docks at Lake Erie, and the two men boarded the boat. As they waited for the steamer to depart, Rulloff jumped up at the last minute and made a dash for the gangway as it was being pulled from the dock. He leapt across the water that lay between the boat and the wharf and quickly disappeared into the crowd gathered on the dock. The escape happened so quickly that Ephriam Schutt was stuck on the boat and had no choice but to go on toward Fairport Harbor alone. There must have been no question in his mind now of the fate of his poor sister.

The town of Madison, Ohio, was located only a few miles east of Fairport Harbor. It was to Madison that Rulloff had addressed his letter to a Mr. Depuy, as this was where his wife was supposed to be living. So Ephriam went on to Madison to see if his sister had ever been there. He described what he found when he arrived in the small Ohio town, saying

"I went to Madison, and inquired for N. Depuy and Mrs. Rulloff; could hear of no such persons; no Mr. Depuy had ever lived there; it was a small place, quite small; I left their names with persons and asked them to write if any such persons were heard from."

Ephriam's hope of ever finding his sister alive must have now been totally lost. From Madison he traveled to Cleveland to obtain a warrant for Rulloff's arrest in Ohio. Rulloff, meanwhile, must have realized that he could not travel back east, for he would soon be caught, so he opted to once again head west. He probably thought it would be best to take the boat to Cleveland rather than getting off at Fairport Harbor, where his brother-in-law might be waiting for him.

Back in Cleveland, Ephriam, now with an Ohio arrest warrant in hand, proceeded to go down to the docks to ask if anyone might have seen Rulloff. Upon his arrival, he noticed two steamers heading into port; both were arriving from the east. He watched as the first boat off-loaded its passengers. Rulloff was nowhere to be seen. The second boat arrived, and once again, Rulloff was spotted with a group of immigrants. Upon seeing his brother-in-law waiting for him, he quickly melted into the crowd and disappeared. This time Ephriam was working with a local law official, and the two went after Rulloff. A short time later they found him hiding behind a dry-goods box in a dockside eating house. The officer approached Rulloff and asked him if his name was Rulloff. Rulloff replied that he was not. Ephriam insisted that it was Rulloff, and he was promptly arrested and taken back to New York in manacles by his persevering brother-in-law. This time Rulloff was returned to Ithaca without incident. The capture of the suspected murderer and Ephriam's heroic manhunt were immortalized for the first time after their return in the September 3, 1845, issue of the Ithaca Journal.

Rulloff's latest visit to Ithaca was spent in the old Ithaca Jail, where he was chained to the floor. Soon he was brought to a hearing before judges Johnson and Day, to see if there was indeed enough evidence to charge him with murder. They concluded that there was and committed him to trial.

Because the bodies of Rulloff's wife and child could not be accounted for, the District Attorney immediately began a search to discover where they might be. All of the evidence pointed to the lake, and it was with considerable manpower and expense that Cayuga Lake was dredged for the bodies. This was no easy task, for the lake's depths reach to over three hundred feet in some locations. It was claimed that this effort cost the taxpayers of

Tompkins County, New York, almost $10,000, which was an enormous sum of money at the time. Over four months was spent trying to locate the bodies and gather enough evidence to put Rulloff on trial for murder; however, the bodies were never discovered. With the search exhausted, the District Attorney realized that there was not sufficient evidence to prove that Rulloff had murdered his wife and child, so he was forced to change his indictment to that of abduction.

Rulloff's trial for the abduction of his wife began in February of 1846. He was represented by S.B. Cushing, a local Ithaca lawyer. The prosecution presented the testimonies of many witnesses, including Rulloff's former neighbors, the Robertsons, many members of the Schutt family, and Dr. Burdick, who first entered the house after Rulloff's disappearance. All of their testimonies supported the abduction theory, although the townspeople felt that Rulloff had committed murder and should be punished for it. This was not possible within the realm of the law, however, and near the end of February 1846, Edward H. Rulloff was found guilty of the abduction of his wife. He was then sentenced to serve ten years in the state prison at Auburn, New York. Rulloff was twenty-six years old and was about to be incarcerated for the second time in his life. Although the people of Ithaca were relieved that Rulloff was now in prison, it must have been a shock to think that the man they once described as being of "more than ordinary learning and acquirements, in all the departments of literature and science..." had now become a reviled murderer.

HE WAS A DICTIONARY HIMSELF

*R*ulloff's time in the state prison at Auburn produced yet another profession to add to his already impressive list of accomplishments. Up until this time he had been a student of law and languages, a pharmacist, a botanical physician, a teacher, and a lecturer of phrenology. This was quite a resume for a man who was only twenty-six years of age and mostly self-educated. Now in prison, he embarked on a new career as a designer of carpets for a local carpet manufacturer by the name of J. Barber & Company. The Barber Company employed a Frenchman who was responsible for the design of the carpets. Somehow Rulloff was assigned as his apprentice, and he apparently picked up the skill of designing rather quickly. Hiram Whiting, a clerk at J. Barber & Company, later recalled the abilities of the incarcerated worker, "[Rulloff] was employed in making patterns and designs for carpets. He was successful in this business, being industrious and ingenious, exhibiting much capacity, tact, and skill."

While he was incarcerated Rulloff also took an interest in the mechanical arts. The workshops of the prison must have helped nurture this newfound curiosity. The policies at the prison provided that a small portion of money could be made from some of the jobs done by the prisoners. Rulloff used the money he earned from his carpet designs to buy many books, mostly dealing with the subject of language. As recalled by a doctor who knew him at the time, "during his prison life...the history of the formation and the philosophy of various languages, especially the Greek, were his constant study, and he acquired an extensive and critical knowledge, not only of the Greek and Latin, but also of the more ancient as well as the modern European tongues." Rulloff was also known to share his love of the classics with some of the people who visited the prison during his internment. According to the doctor, "the students and sometimes the professors of the Auburn Theological seminary at that time held bible classes in Auburn Prison. Rulloff always attended these classes...He amazed and astonished these young men, fresh from their classics, with his knowledge of Greek and Latin as well as the Bible itself. At one time one of them asked if he had a Latin dictionary, to which he replied that he didn't need any, he was a dictionary himself."

Although the claim made by Rulloff that "he was a dictionary himself" may seem arrogant, it was probably not far from the truth. No matter what the circumstances were that surrounded his controversial life, Rulloff indeed possessed a high level of intelligence. This fact was not even disputed by those whose lives were directly affected by his evil wrongdoings.

Rulloff's time in prison almost appeared to be a joyful one, as it allowed him to spend most of his time in carpet design, mechanics, study, and philosophical discussion, but this would soon change. In 1853, Rulloff's seventh year in prison, he began to suffer from an illness, and he became so weakened that he was forced to leave his job as a carpet designer. He was reassigned as a cook for about twenty-five of his fellow inmates; however, his condition worsened and he lost almost eighty pounds. Rulloff recalled his poor health at the time: "I was then so sick that I could not stand up and do the work, but had to sit with my elbows on the table to handle things in cooking, and after washing the dishes I had to lay on the floor on my back and wipe them while resting my elbows on the pavement." Later in life he recalled that the only thing that got him through that terrible time was his desire to survive in order to complete his work on the origin and formations of language.

While he was sick, his captors kept a close watch of his activities, for at first they believed that Rulloff was faking his illness. Eventually they must have become convinced by his declining health and obvious loss of weight, because they finally summoned three different doctors to come and treat him. None of the doctors, however, could find a cause for his ailments, and they too began to suspect that he might be faking his illness in order to shirk his prison duties. This might indeed be the truth, for Rulloff's substantial knowledge of medicine would have certainly aided him if he had needed it.

As Rulloff languished in Auburn, events were occurring in the town of Ithaca that would have surely alarmed him if he had been aware of them. Many people who lived in and around the Ithaca area were still angry over the fact that Rulloff was serving a light sentence for abduction, when he should have been executed for what most citizens believed was a double murder. So obsessed was the town's District Attorney by this outrage that he filed another indictment against Rulloff, once again for the murder of his wife. This indictment had to wait eight more years until Rulloff was due to be released from prison. As the time came near for his release, he eventually learned of this new attempt by the D.A. to put him on trial once again. Rulloff wasted no time and immediately began to study the law to look for a way to block this new indictment.

In January of 1856, Edward Rulloff was released from the state prison at Auburn. As he departed the gates he was greeted by the sheriff of Tompkins County, who presented him with a warrant for his arrest for the murder of his wife. Rulloff showed no emotion as he was put in manacles and brought once again to the old Ithaca Jail. Rulloff had been prepared for this event and continued to work on his own defense while housed in the jail.

At the first hearing for the case, the District Attorney, John Williams, began to use the same evidence which was used to convict Rulloff of his wife's abduction. Rulloff immediately put forward a writ of habeas corpus and demanded that this case be dropped, for he had already been convicted and served his sentence for the crime of abduction. He further argued that the hearing should cease, for it would be representing two adjudications for one offense, commonly known as double jeopardy, or being convicted of the same crime twice. Judge Balcom, who was presiding over this hearing, called District Attorney Williams to his bench. He quietly told him that Rulloff was correct in his assertions, and that it might be better if he indicted Rulloff on the murder of his child, since that charge had not yet been brought to court. The D.A. took the judge's advice and the indictment was promptly changed. Judge Balcom then set a date for the trial for the murder of Rulloff's infant daughter to begin. Rulloff's anger must have reached its pinnacle when he heard this devastating modification. Although his original argument was correct and it was a legal victory, it was short-lived and quickly overshadowed by the new charge which he had not foreseen.

Once again Rulloff found himself back in the Ithaca Jail, mulling over volumes of law books he had borrowed from his newly acquired law team, Boardman and Finch. Francis Finch was the young man who had shared a classroom with Rulloff at the Ithaca Academy when the two studied Greek over eleven years earlier. Finch had recently passed the bar and was just beginning to practice law in Ithaca when his firm took on the Rulloff case.

The next process in preparation for the trial was the selection of an impartial jury. On August 20, 136 prospective jurors were interviewed, the majority of whom said they had formed an opinion in the case. It appeared that it was impossible for Rulloff to receive a fair trial in Tompkins County, because most everyone thought he was guilty. But even before Rulloff heard about the difficulties the lawyers were having in selecting an impartial jury, he was already feverishly looking for a precedent he could cite in order to move the trial out of Tompkins County. He must have realized that he would never be able to obtain a fair trial in Ithaca. He wrote a letter to Francis Finch from his jail cell in which he described a case involving an Italian immigrant who was stabbed. The suspected murderer was subsequently tried in another county because of the notoriety surrounding the case. Rulloff's efforts succeeded, and the trial was relocated to Tioga County.

The trial began in October of 1856 and was presided over by Judge Mason. Rulloff's hope for impartiality apparently had no effect, for it didn't take long for the jury to find him guilty for the murder of his infant daughter. The amazingly resilient Rulloff wasted no time, and at the pronouncement of his sentence, which was death by hanging, he helped his lawyers prepare a bill of exceptions to the ruling of the court. In it they argued that a conviction of murder could not be had when there was not sufficient proof to support the death of his daughter. The court took this bill under consideration and decided to hold their decision until the May General Term of the Supreme Court of New York.

Rulloff was convinced that his argument was legally sound and that his conviction would be overturned. However, the possibility of being executed for the murder of his daughter in a little over six months was not his greatest worry. He had a more immediate fear that revolved around the angry people who lived in Ithaca. Although the trial for his daughter's murder took place in Tioga County, he was still housed in the Ithaca Jail and was periodically brought back and forth from the trial by the sheriff of Tompkins County. The sentiment against Rulloff in Ithaca was so high that he was becoming concerned that he might soon be lynched by an angry mob. An article published in the *Ithaca Journal* during the trial expressed Rulloff's fear as well as the fervor at the time. "But while professing his faith in the law, he has also given utterance to fears that the people might take it into their own heads to have a hanging on their own account, without legal sanction; a fear, entirely unfounded of course because however indignant our citizens might be, they have too much regard for law and order to be participant in such an affair."

Although the local paper proclaimed that the citizens of Ithaca would stay within the boundaries of the law, they greatly underestimated the growing hatred of Rulloff around town and the political fallout that would result from his manipulation of the legal system.

PUT NONE BUT AMERICANS ON GUARD!

*T*he great length of time it took for Rulloff's appeal to come to trial kept him in the Ithaca Jail for over a year. The jail was run by Jacob S. Jarvis, and as a result of Rulloff's lengthy stay there, he got to know the whole Jarvis family. He was soon giving lessons in both language and science to the jailer's eighteen-year-old son, Albert Jarvis. Even though he was accused of two murders, Rulloff's magnetic personality and persuasive speaking must have brought the young Jarvis into his confidence. Albert Jarvis soon became a regular visitor to his father's jail, where he would often sit outside of Rulloff's cell and listen to the knowledgeable man speak. As time went on, the Jarvis boy and Rulloff grew to be good friends. Rulloff must have eventually convinced the young man that it was simply not possible that he was responsible for committing the crimes for which he was being accused. This strange turn of events became public knowledge when the citizens of Ithaca awoke on the morning of May 6, 1857, to the following news report: "Never has our village been thrown into great excitement as on Wednesday morning last when the announcement was made that Rulloff had escaped! Under 7 locks in addition to that which confined him to the floor, the public rested secure in the confidence that whoever else departed from the jail, this prisoner at least was safe, and would be forth coming when wanted."

The town was outraged at the news. Once again the vicious murderer had escaped from Ithaca. Immediately rumors began to circulate that Rulloff had been helped from the inside. The night of his escape, the jailer,

Jacob Jarvis, was summoned by a letter to come immediately to the village of Ovid to aid in the arrest of a Mr. J. Mizner. Jarvis left the jail in the care of his son Albert and a policeman by the name of Milton Ostrander. According to the two men, Rulloff was last seen when they both locked him in his cell that evening.

Later, the exact events of the escape began to unfold as details of what occurred that night were pieced together. A team of black horses was left by a mysterious man in a barn near the town of Corning, New York, approximately forty miles southwest of Ithaca. The team of horses appeared to have been driven very hard and were covered with mud. The man told the owners of the barn that someone would be coming by to pick up the horses in a few days. Eventually, someone arrived. He was described as having long dark hair, a thin face, and a missing right eye. The owner of the barn where the horses were kept began to grow suspicious about what they might have been used for. When he learned of the Rulloff escape, he immediately concluded that the strange men and their team of black horses must have somehow been involved in Rulloff's getaway, although the men were never identified or captured.

It didn't take long for the town to conclude that Albert Jarvis had helped Rulloff break out. An interview with Officer Ostrander the day after the escape revealed facts which led to the suspicion of Albert Jarvis. Ostrander explained that "Rulloff had been shackled to the floor of his cell, and that it would have been impossible for him to remove them and get access to the locks on his cell door, for the shackles were secured with rivets as large as a man's finger."

Rulloff's getaway nearly turned the once peaceful community upside down. Jacob Jarvis was suddenly put under heavy scrutiny for his jail's lack of security and the part that his son was thought to have played in the whole incident. The *Ithaca Journal* ran a story which contained the following revelations about the state of the Ithaca Jail at the time of the breakout: "To show how often appearance passes for that which is not, we may mention that three of the jail locks, each nearly the size of a dining plate were unlocked by a machinist of our village, in the space of less than a minute, on Monday last, without the aid of anything except a crooked wire! Yet in such locks people have confidence and under such have prisoners been kept!"

In the very same issue of the *Ithaca Journal* it was also reported, with no surprise, that Jacob Jarvis had been removed from the position of jailer.

The fervor over the escape of Rulloff didn't stop at harsh criticism of the Ithaca Jail and the family who ran it, for the escape even began to influence the partisan politics of the town:

> Put none but Americans on guard! This sentiment is the corner stone of the Know Nothing Party in this county. It has been carried out, and where is Rulloff? Americans *were* on guard when Rulloff escaped! The Sheriff, Under Sheriff, and Jailer, Constables, Policemen, Police, Justice, [etc.], are all in the hands of the Know Nothings and their party. Into their hands with full confidence in their loud professions, the People placed this convicted murderer. *The People* now demand that he be produced, or that his keepers show by a thorough and rigid judicial investigation of the matter, that they are chargeable with nothing more than gross carelessness. And we will suggest that midnight meetings and examinations before Council, with grips and oaths, digital gyrations, facial grimaces, gammon and flummer won't do. The People are disgusted with such mountebank tricks, and are determined to know who let out Rulloff. And they demand that information of those whose business it was to keep him.

This article was published on the front page of the *Ithaca Journal* shortly after Rulloff's escape. It appears that some politicians have always been able to seize the moment and use it for their own political advantage.

To speak the name Edward Rulloff in the town of Ithaca during this time would probably have prompted a series of varying responses, mostly negative. Some people, however, might have thought it was a blessing that he had escaped, for at least the town was finally rid of this monster.

EVIDENTLY A MAN OF CULTURE
AND EDUCATION

*R*ulloff's escape from the Ithaca Jail must have been arranged because he feared that he might soon be lynched by the angry citizens of Ithaca. He most certainly persuaded young Albert Jarvis to arrange for his escape. Although many writers reported that the Jarvis boy was corrupted by Rulloff, and prior to becoming his student was supposedly a young man of most correct habits and excellent promise, this was far from the truth. Albert Jarvis had been a thief ever since childhood, and he had even once spent time behind bars in the same jail over which his father presided. Jarvis most likely released Rulloff from his cell and arranged to have the mysterious man with one eye and his team of horses whisk Rulloff away on the night of his escape. One cannot, however, lay all the blame on Jarvis, for Rulloff certainly possessed a very persuasive personality. It seems likely that the boy must have admired Rulloff and became convinced that he was being wrongfully accused and should be set free.

While Rulloff was on the run, he may have headed yet again to his brother's home in Clarion, Pennsylvania. It was there he would find a temporary safe haven and might be able to try to piece his life back together. If the theory that his daughter was left in the care of his brother was true, then this reason alone may have drawn him to Clarion. If he did stay at his brother's, his time there must have been short, for soon Rulloff began to search for a place of employment, mainly in the form of a professorship with one of the local colleges. It seems inconceivable to believe that someone who had just escaped from jail and was under suspicion of murdering his wife and child would be out trying to begin a career as a college professor. But that is the essence of Edward Rulloff, and it is exactly what he did.

Rulloff's first attempt at gaining a professorship took place at Jefferson College in the town of Canonsburg, just southwest of Pittsburgh. Jefferson College became one of the first colleges to be established in Western Pennsylvania in 1802. The opening of the college was marked by controversy, as many people affiliated with the new school were devout Presbyterians who were opposed to naming it after the current president, Thomas Jefferson, someone they considered "to be an infidel, a deist, if not atheist, and bitter opposer of the Christian religion."

Rulloff inquired at the college about a position as a teacher in the language department, but there were no openings available. He was probably lucky the college was not hiring at the time, for if its benefactors held such negative sentiments towards Thomas Jefferson, then someone like Edward Rulloff would have most certainly not lasted very long on the faculty.

Next he traveled west to Meadville, Pennsylvania, the home of Allegheny College. Rulloff, now using the alias James Nelson, introduced himself to Dr. John Barker, the fourth president of this small Western Pennsylvania institution that was founded in 1815. Rulloff inquired if there might be a position available for a professor of languages. Dr. Barker proceeded to question Rulloff about his knowledge of the study of language. The meeting between these two scholars lasted for quite some time. Dr. Barker was much impressed with Mr. Nelson (Rulloff), but after their lengthy discussion Barker told him that there were currently no openings in the faculty at his institution. Dr. Barker did, however, present him with a letter of certification. In it he explained that he had examined Mr. Nelson and found him to be knowledgeable in Latin, Greek, Hebrew, French, and German. Dr. Barker also wrote that he found Mr. Nelson to be one of the best linguists it was ever his pleasure to meet.

After his meeting with Dr. Barker, Rulloff wandered through the town of Meadville in search of work. He was told that a local physician, inventor, and naturalist by the name of A.B. Richmond was looking for a mechanic to help him construct a device that he had recently designed. Rulloff sought out Mr. Richmond and introduced himself, once again using the name James Nelson. Mr. Richmond at first thought that Rulloff appeared to be a poor farmer, for his clothes were disheveled and were not those of a gentleman. Rulloff inquired if Mr. Richmond was looking for a partner to help market his new invention. Richmond replied that he indeed was, but that the machine was only in the design stage, and he would need to construct a working model.

As the two men spoke, Richmond came to realize that his first impression was wrong, and that this stranger was indeed an educated man. Rulloff told Richmond that he was a fine mechanic and would be able to construct a working model of the machine. Richmond was very impressed with Rulloff's knowledge, and he agreed to work with him. He offered Rulloff half interest in the patent rights to the machine for the sum of $500. Rulloff accepted this sum and told Richmond that his brother was very wealthy, thus money was no object. For once it appeared that he was telling the truth, for Rulloff's brother, Ruloff Rulofson, was indeed a wealthy man and a highly respected citizen in his town.

After their agreement was set, Mr. Richmond gave Rulloff a tour of his collection room. Richmond was also a refined naturalist who collected many specimens of the natural world, and the two men spent time discussing natural history. When they reached a display of sea shells, Rulloff amazed him with his knowledge of marine invertebrates. Richmond later recalled, "We went into my collection room, and first came to a case containing marine shells. The shells had been lying on cards, and some visitors who had been examining them had [moved] them. He immediately stopped and called my attention to the fact, saying 'Mr. Richmond that is certainly not correct. That shell is not correctly labeled. That shell is surely not *Spondylus Spinosus*, but is the *Argonauti Argo*.' I discovered the mistake, perceiving how it occurred. Of course I was very much astonished to find that he should know anything about them."

Mr. Richmond inquired how this stranger had gained knowledge of marine organisms, to which Rulloff replied that he had an interest in many things. To Richmond's astonishment, their discussion soon turned to the subject of mineralogy as they approached his mineral collection. At every turn, Richmond became more impressed with this man's education. When they arrived at the insect display, Rulloff discussed the field of entomology as if he was indeed a professor of that discipline also. The tour continued, and Rulloff yet again impressed his host, this time with his knowledge of anatomy, as once again recalled by Richmond: "My astonishment increased, when, a little further along, he picked up the skull of an Indian that had been found on a Western battlefield, and remarked, 'Ah, that man received a terrible blow on the right parietal bone. See, it has fractured the tempo-ral bone.' He remarked further, 'He must have been a man of considerable age, as the lambdoidal suture is almost obliterated.'"

The two men next entered into Richmond's laboratory, where he was currently performing an autopsy on a man who had died of arsenic poison-ing. Here Rulloff exhibited his knowledge of chemistry, further amazing his host. Finally, as the tour of the laboratory concluded, Rulloff presented Richmond with the certificate that he had just received from Dr. Barker. Richmond was impressed by the document and taken aback by the notion that not only was this man very well-informed in the subjects of science, but he was also an extremely knowledgeable linguist. Richmond, now thoroughly impressed with the credentials of his guest, told Rulloff that a close friend of his had also recently invented a machine and might require assistance in constructing it. He told Rulloff that he would also be able to do work for him if he so desired.

Later that same day, Richmond introduced Rulloff to his friend, a man by the name of George Stewart. Rulloff entered into an agreement with Stewart under the same circumstances as with Mr. Richmond. When it came time to write up a contract between the two men, Rulloff picked up an old worn pen from Stewart's table and began to write out the terms of their agreement. Mr. Stewart exclaimed that the pen was worn out, and it would not be sufficient. Rulloff replied that it made no difference what he wrote with, for he could write just as well with a stick. Stewart then watched in amazement as he penned, in a beautiful flowing hand, their contract. Amazingly, in the course of one day, Rulloff gained interest in two patents, with two total strangers! This was quite an achievement for a man who was on the run from the law.

It was well known that Edward Rulloff possessed a great understand-ing of law, medicine, and language; however, the recollections of Mr. Richmond reveal other accomplishments of this truly enigmatic man. It is indeed an incredible feat for the human mind to have the ability to speak five or more languages fluently, but to add to this a knowledge of law, medicine, chemistry, and the natural sciences certainly reaches, if not exceeds, the realm of genius. Obviously Rulloff had far surpassed his quest to gain a "general education."

Unfortunately, Rulloff's high level of intelligence failed to help him cope in society. His lifelong quest for knowledge, although it seemed noble at first, turned him into an arrogant and dangerous man. His attitude towards society, which can be inferred from his writings and exploits, was one of disregard. He never seemed to conform to the community in which he resided, always putting himself above the rest, with a fervently self-centered attitude. And as evidenced by how he conducted himself during the time he was under suspicion of murder, he was able to live his life despite the turmoil surrounding him. It was as if he actually thought that he was being wrongfully accused of his crimes. If this is what he truly believed will never be known, but it was certain that the disappearance of his wife and daughter, his escape from jail, and his new life in Pennsylvania were beginning to reveal the complete psychopath that he had become.

For the next few weeks, Rulloff labored on the construction of a working model for Richmond's machine. He preferred to work at night, when Richmond's laboratory was empty, and to sleep during the day. Richmond was very impressed with Rulloff's work, seeing for himself that he indeed was a fine mechanic. Then one day Rulloff was contacted by Dr. Barker of Allegheny College. Barker told him that he had just received a correspondence from the College of Chapel Hill in North Carolina. They were in need of a language teacher and wondered if Dr. Barker knew of anyone who might be interested in the position. He immediately thought of Mr. Nelson (Rulloff) and contacted him right away. Rulloff gladly accepted the offer and made plans to travel south to Chapel Hill.

That same day, Rulloff approached Richmond and told him that he was going to leave town for a few days in order to get the $500 to pay for his portion of the patent rights. He must have been firmly committed to the project and hoped to borrow some money from his brother to assure his stake in the device before he was to leave for North Carolina. Rulloff had also made some handbills that described both Stewart's and Richmond's machines, and he planned to distribute them during his journey to his brother's.

The morning after Rulloff left, news began to spread around town that a local tannery had been broken into and some boots and leather had been stolen. Of course at that time Mr. Richmond would have never suspected that his new business partner had anything to do with the crime. However, it seems likely Rulloff committed the theft in order to help pay for his journey to his brother's.

A few more days had passed since Rulloff's departure when the postmaster in nearby Meadville received a correspondence from the town of Warren, Pennsylvania, which was located north of Meadville. The note described how the jewelry store owned by a Mr. R. P. Bennet of Warren had been broken into and all its contents were stolen. The note further went on to say that the day after the robbery had occurred, the stolen items were found hidden under some logs near the roadside about three miles out of town. The jewelry was wrapped in handbills that advertised a pair of machines that were invented by a Mr. Stewart and a Mr. Richmond. The local authorities now suspected these two men were somehow connected to the burglary. The postmaster awkwardly informed Stewart and Richmond, who were two of the most highly respected men in the town, that they were suspects in the robbery. Both men were outraged at the accusation. Stewart immediately thought of Mr. Nelson, who had made the handbills. He recalled how Nelson had a daguerreotype photo taken of himself recently while in town, so he arranged for a copy of the photo to be sent to the sheriff in Warren. When it was received by the authorities, the man in the photograph was not only connected to the jewelry theft, but was also recognized as the recently escaped murderer from New York, Edward Rulloff. What possible motive Rulloff could have had for wrapping the stolen jewelry in those incriminating handbills will never be known. What is also equally mysterious is why he decided to leave the items behind. Rulloff's plans to travel south were altered, and now he was on the run yet again. As a result, the possibility of him becoming a teacher of language at the College of Chapel Hill would never be realized.

After Rulloff left Warren, he traveled on foot back to New York. It was now the winter of 1858, one of the coldest in years to hit Western New York and Pennsylvania. Rulloff journeyed to Jamestown, New York, which was located on the border of Pennsylvania. When he arrived in Jamestown with a severe case of frostbite in both of his feet, he visited the local drugstore, where he personally prescribed a remedy for his worsening condition. Unfortunately for Rulloff, even his vast knowledge of medicine could not improve his condition, and he was eventually forced to amputate the big toe off his left foot, a procedure he performed himself. He then checked into a local hotel to rest and recover from his surgery.

While Rulloff was recuperating, the darkening shadow of fate once again fell over him. One of the employees at the hotel, who worked in the stable, was a fellow inmate of Rulloff's at Auburn Prison. Upon seeing Rulloff, the former prisoner immediately recognized him as a wanted man. Rulloff must have sensed the man's intentions when he saw him and approached him in the barn near the rear of the hotel. Strangely, Rulloff produced a unique three-barreled pistol, which he had constructed himself, and held it to the head of his former fellow inmate. He told the man not to reveal to anyone who he was, or he would surely kill him. Rulloff realized that he was in danger by being there and immediately fled the area.

One of Rulloff's earlier biographers made the following observation about the fateful meeting in Jamestown between the ex-prisoners: "A promise exacted by a pistol is kept generally no longer than to make sure that the disagreeable weapon will not avenge its violation..." This was indeed true, for not long after Rulloff had left the hotel, the man whom Rulloff had threatened made a visit to the local sheriff. His motivation was not only to save his own life, but also to collect the $1,250 reward that was being offered for information that led to the arrest of Edward Rulloff. The man told Deputy Sheriff James R. Dinnin of his encounter with Rulloff. He also described Rulloff's condition and how he was forced to wear moccasins as a result of his recent amputation. This information would surely help to identify the wanted man and possibly slow down his attempt to leave the area quickly. The sheriff's deputy also learned of the strange three-barreled revolver that Rulloff had in his possession. Dinnin immediately contacted the Ithaca District Attorney with the news and went off in pursuit.

The D. A. informed Dinnin, with good cause, that Rulloff would most likely be heading into Ohio. Therefore, the deputy's first move was to take the train to Cleveland and search for him there. This turned out to be a dead end, so he once again returned to Jamestown. Next, Dinnin received a letter from a man by the name of Lyons, who informed him that Rulloff had been seen in Northern Ohio. Once again Deputy Dinnin traveled to Cleveland. This time he contacted the local authorities and informed them of the situation. Marshal Gallagher, a well known detective in the area, helped Dinnin organize a manhunt. Every policeman in Northern Ohio was alerted, especially those who worked near the railroad stations. Dinnin then began to travel from town to town asking the citizens if they had seen anyone that matched Rulloff's description. He even traveled as far as Toledo, but still nothing turned up.

Finally, two men by the names of McCoy and Curtis who lived south of the port town of Sandusky, Ohio, heard of the manhunt and remembered someone they had seen recently who might fit the description of the wanted man. They remembered his name as being Wilcox, and that he had been teaching at a small writing school outside of Sandusky. McCoy and Curtis tracked down Wilcox at the house of Mr. Smith, who was renting a room to him. When the two men knocked on Mr. Wilcox's door, the man who answered was none other than Edward Rulloff himself. Upon discovering his predicament, Rulloff brandished his odd pistol once again and began to fire shots at the two men. Fortunately for Curtis and McCoy, Rulloff's homemade weapon was not very accurate, and they quickly restrained him. At that point, he surrendered himself peacefully.

Rulloff was brought to the local jail, where he was held until the men could locate Deputy Dinnin. Coincidentally, Dinnin had just arrived at the train station in Sandusky. When he got off the train he noticed a man showing off a strange three-barreled weapon. He immediately recognized that it was similar to the gun Rulloff was known to be carrying. Dinnin approached the man to ask where he acquired such a pistol. It was McCoy who was holding the pistol, and he told Dinnin that it was taken from the infamous fugitive, Edward Rulloff. The sheriff was elated at the news. He introduced himself to McCoy, who was astonished to learn that he was talking to the man he was hoping to locate. Deputy Dinnin happily informed McCoy and Curtis that they would receive a $500 reward for Rulloff's capture. The problem that now confronted Dinnin was the extradition of Rulloff from Ohio. In order to move Rulloff back into New York, he needed to get permission from the governor of Ohio, Salmon P. Chase, who was in Columbus. Dinnin instructed the men to hold Rulloff in the jail at Sandusky until he returned from Columbus with the extradition papers. What happened next was indeed another strange twist in the life of Edward Rulloff.

Apparently, Rulloff's persuasive personality was to yet again take hold; this time it was aimed at the two men whom only hours before he tried to shoot. It appears that Rulloff was becoming concerned about the possibility that he would not be extradited to New York to stand trial. He now felt that the only chance he had at beating his conviction lay in the courts of New York. He was convinced that he had to get out of Sandusky as quickly as possible and return to New York at any cost. Rulloff's bail was set at $1,000, and while he sat in jail awaiting news of his extradition, he convinced his captors to help him return to New York.

A friend of Curtis and McCoy, a man by the name of Smith, somehow convinced the local judge to release Rulloff to his custody for only $500. How Mr. Smith persuaded the judge to lower the bail to $500 and allow Rulloff to be released is not clear. Apparently the local judge did not know who Rulloff was and how much effort had been put into his capture. Or maybe the judge had confidence that Mr. Smith and his friends would see to it that Rulloff was returned to New York under safekeeping, with or without formal extradition papers. Rulloff must have surely bribed Curtis and McCoy into helping him to get out of the Sandusky jail so he could get back to New York. The men paid the bail with the reward money they received for Rulloff's capture and escorted him out of the jail. Before they left for New York, Rulloff led the men to the boarding house where he had been staying, to collect a traveling trunk which held his belongings. In the trunk was approximately $300 or $400 in gold, along with some incriminating papers.

McCoy, Curtis, and Smith then traveled to Ithaca with Rulloff in custody. When they arrived, Rulloff and his trunk were handed over to the Ithaca District Attorney. Upon searching the trunk, the D.A. discovered that the gold and the papers were gone. Unknown to Rulloff and his escorts, the contents of the trunk were already known by the Ithaca District Attorney, because Deputy Dinnin had discovered what it contained when he searched Rulloff's room shortly after he had been apprehended. In a correspondence to the District Attorney, Dinnin explained that the trunk not only contained gold, but also some written information pertaining to those who had helped him escape from the Ithaca Jail. The three men from Ohio were now suspected of allowing Rulloff to dispose of possible evidence that the papers in the trunk may have contained in exchange for the gold. They were also demanding a $500 reward for Rulloff's capture. Unfortunately, the evidence to suggest that McCoy, Curtis, and Smith allowed Rulloff to destroy possible evidence was extremely circumstantial, and the D.A. was inclined to pay them the reward.

Ironically, just as this decision was made, another man from Ohio, Peter Bardshire, arrived in Ithaca claiming the reward for Rulloff's capture. Who Peter Bardshire was and how he explained to have the right to claim the reward is unknown. To add to the confusion, the citizens of Ithaca began to demand that Deputy Dinnin be the one to receive the reward. Eventually, it was decided that Curtis, McCoy, and Smith, although under suspicious circumstances, were entitled to $500 for the return of Rulloff to New York. Deputy Dinnin also received a $500 reward granted by the governor of New York for the role he played in the capture. Apparently Mr. Bardshire received nothing. With this resolved, yet another strange chapter in Rulloff's life was concluded.

PICTURE ALBUM

Small portrait of Edward H. Rulloff

Drawing of Edward H. Rulloff published in the Phrenological Journal and Life Illustrated *magazine, September 1871*

EDWARD H. RULLOFF.

*The children of Ruloff Rulofson, Edward H. Rulloff's brother, circa 1900.
Rear: William R. Rulofson, Priscilla Jane Stratton, Jeannette A. McCaslon.
Front: Elizabeth B. Clover, Merta H. Hoover. Priscilla Jane Stratton may
actually be Edward Rulloff's child who was presumed murdered in 1845.*

STOP THE MURDERER!

$1,250 REWARD!

On the night of the 5th of May 1857, *EDWARD H. RULLOFF*, convicted of the murder of his infant daughter, **escaped from the Jail** in this village. He was assisted in his escape by some person or persons outside of the Jail. Said Rulloff is about 5 feet 8 inches high, stout built, short thick neck, large head, a man of quick, precise motions, and stoops forward when he walks, speaks English, German, and other languages, and had a beard of some six or eight weeks growth when he left, weighs about 180 lbs. measures round the chest 40 inches, round the waist 37 or 38 inches, broad between the eyes, dark brown hair, rather small, dark blue, or hazel eyes, broad full face, probably some callouses on his ancles caused by shackles. He was a convict in Auburn prison for ten years for the abduction of his wife.

Late on the evening of the 5th of May, a team was seen standing near the jail, described as follows:

Off Horse, color dark brown or black, hollow back, 15 hands high, good front, high headed, prompt, small white spot above the eyes, and a little to the off side of the head, a small white spot, one and a half inches long and a half inch wide, about 3 inches below the eyes in center of the head, white spot on the back from pads to harness, a little white just above the hoof on the near hind foot, probably 12 years old or upwards, switch tail natural length, which the horse carries up pretty well.

Near horse, black, small star in farhead, 15 hands high, white spot on back from pads to harness, switch tail, natural length, probably about 12 years old. Both horses have heavy manes.

The harness on the horses was a light, two horse harness, silver plated, web lines with round tips, hip straps round, light pads, horse-shoe buckles, under side of collars russet collar, outside black, square blinds to bridles.

[illegible text] Buggy, whiffletrees and neck yoke painted [illegible] blue. A brass leather 5 or 6 inches wide and 7 or 8 inches long runs round the center of the neck yoke stiched, with a hole in the leather [illegible] run on of that leather and three screws run through the leather into the neck yoke. Iron axletrees to the buggy, open seat, small iron or brass running through the [illegible] seat trimmed with enameled cloth, [illegible] and neck to buggy over wood, oil cloth apron, buggy painted a reddish brown, with red striper, pole of the buggy black, but paint somewhat worn off.

There was with this buggy and team a black India Rubber or Gum Over Coat, one of the Union Company's manufacture in N. Y. city Goodyear's patent, on the lining of which are the letters N[illegible] or N.sh probably a coat mark.

On the morning of the 6th of May, at 8 o'clock the said team, buggy and Gum Coat were driven into the village of Corning, about 40 miles from this place. The team was very sweaty and tired, and covered completely with mud, as also were the buggy and coat. The man who drove the team was about 5 feet 8 inches tall, light whiskers, of light color, brown hair, with ordinary silk hat, and dark clothes, and called his name I. Allen. He ordered the team put in the barn and not to be taken out until he sent or called for them.

[repeated/duplicate descriptive text]

The harness on the horses was a light, two horse harness, silver plated, web lines with round tips, hip straps round, light pads, horse-shoe buckles, under side of collar russet collar, outside black, square blinds to bridles.

[illegible] Buggy, whiffletrees and neck yoke painted [illegible] blue. A brass leather 5 or 6 inches wide and 7 or 8 inches long runs round the center of the neck yoke stiched, with a hole in the leather [illegible] of the leather, and three screws run through the leather into the neck yoke. Iron axletrees to the buggy, open seat, small iron or brass running through the [illegible] seat trimmed with enameled cloth, [illegible] and neck to buggy over wood, oil cloth apron, buggy painted a reddish brown, with red striper, pole of the buggy black, but paint somewhat worn off.

There was with this buggy and team a black India Rubber or Gum Over Coat, one of the Union Company's manufacture, on the lining of which are the letters N[illegible] or N.sh probably a coat mark.

On the morning of the 6th of May, at 8 o'clock the said team, buggy and Gum Coat were driven into the village of Corning, about 40 miles from this place. The team was very sweaty and tired, and covered completely with mud, as also were the buggy and coat. The man who drove the team was about 5 feet 8 inches tall, light whiskers, of light color, brown hair, with ordinary silk hat, and dark clothes, and called his name I. Allen. He ordered the team put in the barn and not to be taken out until he sent or called for them. He said he would send or call for the team in 3 or 4 days, and went off.

About 10 days after the team was left in Corning, a man calling himself James Henry called for the team, with a bill of sale purporting to be executed by Isaac Allen, and an order for the team signed, by Isaac Allen, and dated Cuba, Allegany Co., N. Y., May 11th, 1857. This Henry is a man about 5 feet 6 or 8 inches tall, weighs about 150, dark brown hair, not quite black, rather long featured, hollow cheeks, good sized head, not very high but full forehead, his right eye out, left eye rather prominent; blue or grey, and about 25 or 30 years old.

Any information concerning the former or present owners of this team, buggy and coat, the former history of the said James Henry, and particularly respecting the present or former history or whereabouts of the said Allen, addressed to the subscriber, Sheriff of Tompkins Co., at Ithaca, N. Y. will be thankfully received and will promote the ends of public justice. A reward of **$250** is hereby offered for such information as shall lead to the conviction of any person or persons who aided in the escape of the said Edward H. Rulloff, and a further reward of **$500** is offered for the return of the said Rulloff to the [illegible] of this county.

The above described Team, Buggy and Coat, are now in the possession of the subscriber.

Ithaca, N. Y. May, 29, 1857.   **R. J. IVES**, *Sheriff of Tompkins County.*

Proclamation,

By John A. King, Governor of the State of New York:

Information having been communicated to me by R. J. Ives, Sheriff of the county of Tompkins, and by other respectible residents of that county, that *Edward H. Rulloff*, convicted of the murder of his infant daughter, had escaped from the Jail at Ithaca, with a request that a reward should be offered by me for the apprehension of said *Rulloff* in addition to the reward offered by the said Sheriff. I do therefore hereby offer a reward of **Five Hundred Dollars** to any person who shall give information which shall lead to the apprehension of the said *Rulloff.*

In Witness whereof, I have hereunto affixed my name and the Privy Seal of the State, the twelfth day [S. L.] of June, in the year of our Lord one thousand eight hundred and fifty-seven.

By the Governor,

Henry I. Seaman, *Private Secretary.*   JOHN A. KING.

A copy of the reward poster for the capture of Edward Rulloff issued by the Tompkins County Sheriff shortly after Rulloff's escape from the Ithaca Jail in May of 1857

SHALL THE

Murderer Go Unpunished!

EDWARD H. RULLOFF will soon gain his freedom unless prompt and effective measures are taken by the people to prevent it. It is confidently believed that the new trial that has been ordered by the Court of Appeals will not be had, but on the contrary it is the intention to *Secretly Smuggle* this atrocious *Murderer* out of the country, where he will be set at liberty, to add fresh victims to the number he has already sent unannounced before their GOD. Since his confinement he has repeatedly threatened that if he is once more a free man, he will seek satisfaction in the *Blood* of the relatives of the *Murdered* wife. Shall these things be? Shall this *Monster* be turned loose to glut his tiger appetite for Revenge and Blood? Shall the Ends of JUSTICE BE DEFEATED? We trust not! We hope not! We implore you, citizens of Tompkins County, let it not go out to the world, that there can be no JUSTICE had in your midst! In the name of HUMANITY, in the name of the relatives of the *murdered* wife, whose heart-strings have been lacerated by this *Fiend* in human shape, in the name of the Murdered wife and child, whose pale ghost calls to you from the silent tomb to do your duty, we ask you---SHALL THE MURDERER GO UNPUNISHED? Shall we let this convicted felon *escape*? Will you allow Edward H. Rulloff to breathe the same pure air of freedom we enjoy? Will you allow this man, who bears the mark of *Cain* upon his brow, to go forth in this community and add fresh victims to the grave? NO, you will not! You cannot!

We call on those who wish JUSTICE done to the *Murderer* to meet at the CLINTON HOUSE in Ithaca on Saturday, March 12th, 1859, at 12 o'clock, noon. It will depend on the action you take that day whether Edward H. Rulloff *walks forth a free man, or whether he dies the death he so richly deserves.* MANY CITIZENS.

Shall the Murderer Go Unpunished! flyer, March 9, 1859

*Facsimile of a photograph taken of William Dexter (right)
and Albert Jarvis (left) shortly after their bodies were
pulled from the Chenango River in 1871*

Etching of Edward H. Rulloff

*Edward H. Rulloff's death mask which was cast shortly after
his execution in Binghamton, New York, May 1871.
The actual cast is currently on display at the
History Center in Ithaca, New York.*

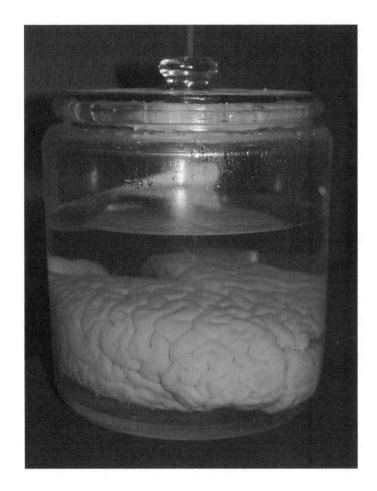

Rulloff's brain on display in Uris Hall, Cornell University,
as part of the Wilder Brain Collection

SICKENED AND SATISFIED

*W*hile Rulloff was on the run in Pennsylvania, his sentencing for the murder of his daughter had been postponed. When he was returned to Ithaca from Ohio in March of 1858, he was once again held in the old Ithaca Jail. Almost immediately he began to work on his case. His sentencing was now scheduled to take place in May, in the nearby town of Elmira. Rulloff began to correspond with his attorneys about how they should proceed with his case. He wrote to them from his cell almost every day, giving them legal advice which he thought would be helpful. A perfect example of how Rulloff assisted his attorneys during this time can be found in a letter he sent to them in late March of 1858, in which he wrote:

Gentlemen,

Edward R. Boyle, Esq. of N.Y. City, Attorney-at-Law, to all appearance a gentlemen, and practitioner of no little repute, told me that within a year it has been decided by Court of Appeals of this state that <u>in criminal cases Circuit Courts have no jurisdiction</u> and that in consequences a new trial was granted in the case of an Italian charged with stabbing a man in N.Y. City and tried before a Circuit judge in a neighboring county...if without jurisdiction, my conviction was void not merely irregular or erroneous but absolutely void, and of no authority whatever in law...

Further on in this same letter, Rulloff instructed his lawyers to look more closely into this matter and possibly travel to New York City to see the attorney he had mentioned. From the surviving documents that pertain to Rulloff's case, it is evident that Rulloff provided many in-depth scenarios which his counsel could use to their advantage.

Many of the letters which Rulloff wrote in prison were written on used pieces of writing paper. This is evidenced by a note he wrote to his attorneys during the time of his appeal which was on the back of a letter he received from his old employer W.C. Barber, the carpet maker, which read in part:

EH Rulloff,

> Your order was only just received owing to my absence from town. Enclosed I hand you a note on Tompkins County [bank] for fifty dollars. I have some new patterns 4 or 5 which I wish you to copy as soon as possible. Don't make any other engagements until these are done for me. I will bring you the patterns, design paper & paint on Monday...

This letter proves that Rulloff was once again at work designing carpets. He must have contacted Mr. Barber for the purpose of raising money to pay for his defense. This also suggests that Rulloff was successful at his design work, for Barber would have to travel the forty some miles from Auburn to do business with Rulloff, and a fifty dollar advance was no small sum of money to be paid in 1858, especially if you were a suspected murderer housed in the local jail.

Rulloff was represented once again by the law firm of Boardman and Finch. His principle attorney at the time was Joshua Spencer, a highly esteemed lawyer with the firm. Using Rulloff's argument to dismiss the case on the grounds that the Circuit Court did not have jurisdiction over it, his attorneys issued a writ of error and motioned to have the case brought before the Court of Appeals. Even in the mid-eighteen hundreds, court proceedings moved slowly, and Rulloff's case wasn't brought before the Court of Appeals until May of 1858. Rulloff's other counsel, Francis M. Finch, traveled to Albany to argue the case. After waiting two months for this opportunity, Finch appeared before the court and was told that they refused to hear the appeal on the grounds that sentencing for Rulloff's conviction had not been completed by the Circuit Court. The writ of error was dismissed, and Finch returned to Ithaca after traveling all the way to Albany for nothing. Rulloff, upon hearing the outcome of his appeal, wrote to Finch that he "was sickened and satisfied." He was obviously sickened by the defeat of his writ of error, but his satisfaction lay in his ability to appeal the decision, as expressed by an article published in the *Ithaca Journal* at the time that reported "the sentence will doubtless be pronounced at the next July term of the court at Delhi. A new Writ of Error will then doubtless be sued out, and the case will be heard in the court of Appeals September next."

And so it was for Edward Rulloff that in July of 1858, he appeared in Delhi, New York, at the general term of the Supreme Court. Presiding over the sentencing was Judge Gray, who took only a few minutes to set down the sentence of death by hanging. The execution was to take place in the town of Owego, New York, on August 27, 1858, between the hours of 10:00 A.M. and 2:00 P.M. The judge then asked the prisoner if he had any remarks to add. Rulloff rose from his chair and began a speech which lasted for over a half hour. Using technical legal language and quoting various decisions and precedents, Rulloff made three demands. His first he had previously written about to his lawyers. He moved that the case be dismissed on the grounds that the court did not have jurisdiction to decide it. He argued that the *certiorari* (writ of a superior court to call up the records of an inferior court) was erroneous, because the Special Terms Court had no authority in criminal cases. Rulloff then argued a second point for dismissal. He explained that the decision reached by the three justices of the Supreme Court infringed on his right to a fair trial by an impartial jury, because Judge Mason had presided over the circuit court in Owego and was also one of three Superior Court judges in Binghamton. Rulloff claimed that "the same law that secures to parties, an impartial jury, secures them an appellate tribunal, whose minds are unbiased, and whose pride of opinion shall not be concerned in upholding in Superior Court, the opinion they may have expressed in a court below."

With the tone of a seasoned trial attorney, Rulloff concluded his statement by making a third objection to the ruling, stating that his case was decided by the Superior Court in Binghamton when he was not present. He told the court, "The last constitution provides that in any trial in any court whatever, the party accused *shall be allowed to appear* and defend in person. To hold a person bound by any judicial proceeding when he is involuntarily absent would be bad enough, but to lock him up and deny him the privilege of attending, is *tyranny* unknown to the law."

Rulloff's performance in the courtroom certainly shows a great knowledge of the law, along with a lawyer's flair for using it to his advantage. The court took his comments under consideration and adjourned for the day. One week later, Rulloff returned to the courtroom to hear the decision regarding his grounds for dismissal. The court denied his objections and proceeded to sentence him to death by hanging once again. Rulloff immediately filed for an appeal, which the court accepted. Once again he had put off his execution by utilizing his knowledge of the American legal system.

While Rulloff waited in the Ithaca Jail for his appeal to proceed, a young boy by the name of Sam Halliday visited the jail to get a look at the infamous man. Halliday grew up to become a prominent lawyer in Ithaca. Later in his life, he delivered a famous lecture about Edward Rulloff. The following is his boyhood account of meeting Rulloff in jail: "I went to the Tompkins County [Ithaca] Jail with my oldest brother. I expected to see a monster in human form. In fact, I was a little timid about going at all. It was a long time before I could be convinced that the gentlemanly and mild mannered man that I saw in the cell was Rulloff, the murderer. One thing impressed me; it was the way in which he carried his head, a little to one side in not a coy but a gentle, winning and winsome manner, while his voice was gentleness itself."

Halliday's childhood description of Rulloff matched that of most of the people who knew him at the time. One could easily be held in awe of someone who possessed such intelligence, and a gentle, persuasive manner. If not for his criminal tendencies, Rulloff could have easily been regarded as a great man.

Rulloff's appearance in the Court of Appeals was set for March of 1859, and as he continued to prepare for his case, tragedy struck his law team. His principle lawyer up until this time, Joshua Spencer, a highly respected Utica lawyer who was part of the firm of Boardman and Finch, died shortly before Rulloff's Court of Appeals appearance. Both Spencer and Rulloff had thought that his best defense would be not to attack the validity of the power of the Supreme Court to decide the case, which Rulloff had argued earlier, but to instead argue that Rulloff could not be convicted of his daughter's murder because of the lack of sufficient evidence to prove that she was indeed dead. Their new angle was based on the legal principle of *corpus delecti*, which literally means "the body of the offense." Both Rulloff and Spencer believed that to convict an individual of murder, it was necessary to prove that the murder occurred by producing the body of the alleged victim, or a portion thereof, and that a murder could not be established by circumstantial evidence alone. This legal view was put forth in an early decision made in England by Lord Hale, who wrote, "No person should be convicted of murder unless the fact were proved to be done, or at least the body found."

Francis Finch did not agree with this line of attack, however. He felt that the Hale ruling was too vague when it stated "unless the fact proved to be done." Spencer and Rulloff dismissed Finch's opinion, thinking he was too young and inexperienced to know how best to appeal the case, and his opinions were ignored. The death of Spencer was a hard blow to Rulloff, who now had to find a new lawyer to argue his case. He instructed Finch to contact Nicholas Hill, a prominent Albany lawyer. Hill looked over the case, but his fee was so high that Rulloff could not retain his services. His only option now was Francis M. Finch. Finch, however, still held a strong belief in arguing the case his own way. Eventually the two stubborn men found common ground, and they worked together to try to best prepare their defense. The young lawyer felt confident with the legal brief he was preparing. Rulloff finally agreed to give Finch total control, and Finch traveled to Albany once again, ready to present his case.

The representative for the people against Rulloff was former United States Senator Daniel Dickenson, who was a highly respected prosecutor. Finch arrived in Albany and on the day of the appeals trial ran into the lawyer who Rulloff originally wanted to represent him, but could not afford, Nicholas Hill. Hill told Finch not to worry about his case, for he was right in his appeal. This must have given Finch a boost of confidence, for his performance that day would be unforgettable. Finch's argument began by acknowledging that it was not necessary for a murder to be proven by producing a body, and that it was entirely possible for a killing to be established by circumstantial evidence. Finch then stated that, "if the murder of the infant Rulloff had been proved, and that her death was established as perpetrated by her own father, then Edward Rulloff would indeed be guilty; however, the mere absence of Rulloff's daughter is not so strong and intense to produce the full assurance of moral certainty...to establish death." Finch then continued to utilize common law precedents to support his argument. Up until this time, the courts in New York State had not ruled on the interpretation of *corpus delecti*, and the young Francis M. Finch would become monumental in helping to define its legal interpretation.

At the end of Finch's argument, the prominent prosecutor, Dickenson, began his argument for the people. His main points were the very same ones which Finch had already stated. The court interrupted Dickenson and said that the defense had already agreed to those points. The court then proceeded to ask if the prosecution had anything to add about the absence of a body as sufficient evidence to warrant proof of murder. Dickenson was not prepared for Finch's brilliant defense and was caught off guard. He soon sat down and closed the People's case. After deliberation, the Court of Appeals recalled the prosecution and defense and delivered the following monumental opinion:

> To warrant a conviction of murder, there must be direct proof, either of the death, as by the finding and identification of the corpse, or of criminal violence adequate to produce death and exerted in such a manner as to account for the disappearance of the body. The corpus delecti in murder has two components, death as the result and the criminal agency of another as the means. It is only when there is direct proof of one that the other can be established by circumstantial evidence. The rule as to direct proof must be regarded as part of the humane policy of the common law that many guilty should escape rather than one innocent suffer.

The ruling of the court was to reverse the decision of the lower courts unless the prosecution possessed other evidence than the absence of Rulloff's daughter as proof of her murder. There was no further evidence, and Rulloff was acquitted. It is interesting to observe the way the court presented its decision, for they must have believed that Rulloff was most likely the cause of his daughter's disappearance, but lacked the evidence to prove it, when they ended their written decision with the statement, "many guilty should escape rather than one innocent suffer." Whatever the hidden message, Rulloff was once again a free man, thanks to the help of the young lawyer, Francis M. Finch. This was the just the beginning of a great career for Finch, who later became a trustee of Cornell University, Judge of the Court of Appeals for the State of New York, Dean of the Cornell Law School, and author of *The Blue and the Gray*, an epic poem of the American Civil War, and *His Side of the Story*, a lengthy poem about the life of Edward Rulloff.

News traveled much slower in 1859 than today, but gradually the citizens of Ithaca learned of Finch's grand legal presentation and became alarmed at the possibility that Rulloff would be set free. On the morning of March 9, 1859, a handbill was circulated throughout the Ithaca area, which read as follows:

Shall The Murderer Go Unpunished!

Edward H. Rulloff will soon gain his freedom unless prompt and effective measures are taken by the people to prevent it. It is confidently believed that the new trial ordered by the Court of Appeals will not be had, but on the contrary it is the intention to *Secretly Smuggle* this atrocious *Murderer* out of the country, where he will be set at liberty, to add fresh victims to the number he has already sent unannounced before their GOD. Since his confinement he has repeatedly threatened that if he is once more a free man, he will seek satisfaction in the *Blood* of the relatives of the *Murdered* wife. Shall these things be? Shall this *Monster* be turned loose to glut his tiger appetite for Revenge and Blood? Shall the ends of JUSTICE be defeated? We trust not! We hope not! We implore you, citizens of Tompkins County, let it not go out into this world, that there can be no Justice had in our midst! In the name of HUMANITY, in the name of the relatives of the *murdered* wife, whose heart-strings have been lacerated by this *fiend* in human shape, in the name of the murdered wife and child, whose pale ghost calls to you from the silent tomb to do your duty, we ask you— SHALL THE MURDERER GO UNPUNISHED! Shall we let this convicted felon *escape*? Will you allow this man, who bears the mark of *Cain* upon his brow, to go forth in this community and add fresh victims to the grave? NO, you will not! You cannot! We call on those who wish JUSTICE done to the *Murderer* to meet at the CLINTON HOUSE in Ithaca on Saturday, March 12th,

1859, at 12 o'clock, noon. It will depend on the action you take that day whether Edward H. Rulloff *walks forth a free man, or whether he dies the death he so richly deserves*. [signed] MANY CITIZENS.

The fears that Rulloff once had about being lynched by the angry citizens of Ithaca, which prompted him to escape jail almost three years earlier, seemed to be resurfacing in a much bolder fashion. This leaflet began to cause a stir in the Ithaca area, and it appeared that the peaceful citizens of Ithaca were amassing into an angry mob. So serious was their intent, that a large battering ram, constructed of a full-grown pine log and equipped with handles and a metal ring to prevent it from splitting, was constructed for the purpose of breaking into the jail. This battering ram was hidden in the Six Mile Gorge, not far from the jail. The fervor which was sweeping through the town over this affair was once again expressed by the *Ithaca Journal*:

> Have those instrumental in calling this meeting fully considered the consequences? Have they accounted the cost of an attempt to storm the jail, when the law makes it imperative on the Sheriff to defend it with all the force which he is empowered to call to assist him? If they have not, it is time they looked the matter square in the face. We are not speaking of the guilt or innocence of Rulloff, and certainly are no friend of his, but declare it is our conviction that those who advise and participate in this movement are more dangerous members of society than even Rulloff himself. It would be a disgrace to our village and county should such a meeting be held, from which we could not for long years recover. If laws are wrong correct them by proper means; but to subvert and over turn them by mob is more to be deprecated than ought else beside...

The lawful plea put forth by the editors of the *Ithaca Journal* was indeed a noble gesture; however, the situation had already gotten out of control. When Francis Finch returned to Ithaca, he was unaware of the trouble that had been brewing in his hometown, and after the elation of his recent legal victory in Albany subsided, he once again settled into his old routine. The afternoon of March 12, 1859, brought Mr. George Schuyler to the law offices of Boardman & Finch to warn the two lawyers of the mob that was gathering at the front of the grand old hotel called the Clinton House, located in downtown Ithaca. He told Finch that two thousand citizens had gathered there, and a meeting was being held in reference to the hanging of Edward Rulloff. The angry mob was organized by Augustus Phillips of Ithaca. Many citizens, including the father of Rulloff's wife, spoke to the gathering mob. The main message of the meeting was that Rulloff should be hanged as soon as he could be caught. The battering ram was readied, along with the hanging rope. Boardman and Finch normally took lunch at the Clinton House, but Mr. Schuyler warned them to do otherwise on this day. Finch agreed, but the elder Boardman would do no such thing. He believed that they had only performed their duty as attorneys and should not be afraid of the gathering. The two lawyers walked to the Clinton House for lunch and found the mob preparing for the worst. The two men were untouched, but the air around them was filled with violent talk and angry gestures.

On the day prior to these extraordinary events, Sheriff Robertson, who was in charge of Rulloff's incarceration at the Ithaca Jail during his appeal, was fully aware of the trouble that was brewing in town. The sheriff knew what was expected to happen the very next day. In an attempt to prevent such a violent action by the town's citizens, he asked for assistance from the local volunteer militia, the Dewitt Guards, to help him fend off any attempt by the mob to break into the jail and apprehend Rulloff. The Dewitt guards declined his offer, although this was later disputed by a spokesman for the group who said that if they had been called to action, they would have done so without hesitation. If this was mere damage control or the actual truth is not known. Sheriff Robertson, however, was able to covertly transport Rulloff to Auburn Prison without their help and without the knowledge of the people of Ithaca.

After the mob had gathered at the Clinton House and all of the rallying speeches were delivered, three men were chosen to go and retrieve Rulloff. Shortly thereafter, it was learned that the sheriff had taken Rulloff to Auburn. It might seem that this fact alone would have dispersed the angry crowd; however, the organizers of the mob continued to persevere and now took up a collection to pay for the expenses of three men designated to travel to Auburn and bring Rulloff back.

Eventually the crowd began to disperse, and later the whole affair was called off; however, feelings towards the Sheriff Robertson were at an all-time low. Many citizens felt that Sheriff Robertson should be brought up on formal charges for illegally removing Rulloff to another county. The *Ithaca Journal* once again sided with the law and reported that Robertson "acted from proper motives and in what he deemed a correct discharge of his duties."

As the days passed after Rulloff's removal, the town of Ithaca slowly began to settle back to its normal routine. Sheriff Robertson was never formally charged for his actions, but unfortunately became the scapegoat toward which the mob anger had been vented. His unpopularity was so high that he had to seek affirmation of his duty from high office in the State of New York to publicly clear his name, as was also reported in the *Ithaca Journal*. "The Rulloff excitement appears to have entirely subsided in our village, and we suppose it has elsewhere. Sheriff Robertson returned on Thursday last, having his absence conferred with the Attorney General, the Governor, and the Adjutant General, all of whom, without hesitancy unqualifiedly approved of his removing Rulloff."

Rulloff remained in Auburn Prison until his appeal was formally received by the Ithaca District Attorney. Meanwhile, the D.A. was also busy preparing to file charges pertaining to Rulloff's escape from jail, as well as his possible responsibility for the deaths of his brother-in-law's wife and daughter. Nearly fifteen years earlier, Mrs. Schutt and her new-born infant died shortly after the baby was born; both had been treated by Rulloff, who was acting as their doctor. The Schutt family was becoming suspicious of their deaths and wondered if Rulloff had indeed murdered them also. The District Attorney ordered that the bodies, or what remained of them after fifteen years, be exhumed and analyzed to determine if they might have been poisoned by Rulloff. Because of the length of time they had spent in the ground, it was nearly impossible to perform a complete autopsy, and only portions of what were believed to be Mrs. Schutt's stomach were sent to a doctor by the name of Dormeus to be examined. His subsequent report reveled that there were traces of copper compounds found in the tissue; however, they were not in sufficient amounts to be pronounced the definite cause of her death. The copper traces could have been introduced into her body from the soil in which she was buried or from her decomposing coffin. The deaths of Mrs. Schutt and her infant daughter were most likely the result of the poor medical knowledge of the time and not by poisoning, as the Schutts now believed. The autopsy revealed that there was not sufficient evidence to convict Rulloff of their murders.

The judgment by the Court of Appeals stated that should more evidence be found by the prosecution to convict Rulloff, he could be retried at the next term of the Supreme Court. Although at the time the prosecution had no new evidence, they used the suspected murders of Mrs. Schutt and her daughter as means to hold Rulloff in prison until the autopsy report was completed. Technically Rulloff was a free man, but he had to languish in jail, waiting for the next session of the court in May of 1859. When the time finally arrived, the prosecution failed to produce new evidence to convict Rulloff of either the murder of his own daughter or the murders of his sister-in-law and niece; however, the prosecution did manage to have Rulloff tried for his escape from jail. The court quickly found him guilty of this offense and sentenced him to one year. Rulloff once again was returned to the prison at Auburn to serve his time. Of course he immediately began to appeal his sentence, this time using unique legal terminology concerning the concept of a jail break, which he expressed to Francis Finch: "the difference between 'breach of prison' or 'breaking jail' is only committed when the prisoner himself breaks the jail and effects his own escape…when jail is broken or the prisoner is set at large by some other persons is one of "voluntary escape" if done by the jailer…" It seemed that Rulloff was claiming that the jailer's son, Albert Jarvis, was responsible for his escape!

Rulloff's opinion of his "voluntary escape" is an interesting legal argument, which must have impressed Finch of his client's resourcefulness. He was trying to convince the court that his escape from jail was not his own design, but that of the jailer's son. He further argued that his escape was justified in order to prevent him from being lynched by the angry citizens of the town. Rulloff tried to prove to the court that his life was in danger and that his escape was the only way to save it. He certainly possessed a talent for presenting unique legal arguments, although by the time his appeal reached the court, his year in jail had almost come to an end and the matter was promptly dropped.

Edward Rulloff was released from Auburn Prison in the spring of 1860, but much to his dismay he was immediately seized by officers from Warren, Pennsylvania. The Ithaca District Attorney had notified the authorities in Warren that Rulloff was about to be set free. The D.A. may have lost all his chances for trying to convict Rulloff in New York, but while he was on the run in Pennsylvania, Rulloff was suspected of robbing a jewelry store. As soon as he stepped out of the prison at Auburn, Rulloff was taken into custody and brought to Pennsylvania, where he was held until his case could be brought to trial. Once again Rulloff used his legal knowledge to gain his own freedom. He argued that the hearsay evidence of the case was not sufficient to detain him, and he should be set free on bail. The only evidence to connect Rulloff to the robbery lay in the handbills in which the stolen goods were found to be wrapped. He argued that if this was the only evidence they had, then his partners for whom he made the leaflets, Mr. Richmond and Mr. Stewart, should also be jailed and tried. The judge begrudgingly accepted Rulloff's argument and he was released on bond. He fled Pennsylvania immediately, never to return.

Edward Rulloff was once again a free man; however, his past troubles had cost him fifteen years of his life, and undoubtedly could have resulted in his own execution had it not been for his brilliant manipulation of the law. Although Francis Finch's masterful argument was monumental in reversing Rulloff's case and winning his appeal, it is known from the volumes of letters written to Finch from Rulloff while in jail that he also played a major role in helping win his own freedom. As a result of Rulloff's case, New York State law was forever changed, and the term *corpus delicti* would be added to the vocabulary of many citizens who resided in Central New York.

The disappearance of Rulloff's wife and daughter and the events which surrounded it most certainly point to Rulloff's guilt; however, his perseverance allowed him to walk away free. During the time period after Rulloff's escape from the Ithaca Jail, he endured life as a fugitive from the law twice, almost became a college professor, secured interest in two patents, amputated his own toe, survived the threat of being lynched by an angry mob, was accused and eventually acquitted of the murder of his wife, his daughter, his sister-in-law, and his niece, spent time in jail for his escape, and finally faced and eventually evaded the charge of robbery in Pennsylvania. In the face of all this turmoil, he managed to wage a legal battle which would help set an important legal precedent. Most condemned men who faced such insurmountable odds would surely have given up, but Rulloff proved to be more than able to take up the challenge and use the law to his advantage to gain his acquittal. If Rulloff's life story had ended at this point, he would still have been remembered as a uniquely intelligent person who manipulated the law with a surgeon's precision. But his extraordinary life was far from over.

AND YET A THIEF!

As previously stated, Rulloff left Erie, Pennsylvania, in the fall or summer of 1860 to evade conviction for his alleged robbery. What he did for the following year is unknown. On November 20, 1861, however, it is quite clear what Rulloff was up to, for this is the date that he was sentenced to three years in the Sing Sing Correctional Facility located at Ossining, New York, approximately thirty miles north of New York City. Rulloff was convicted on the charge of robbery in the third degree. It seems incredible that Rulloff, after so many years tirelessly trying to free himself from his internment, would end up in prison a little over a year after his great legal victory.

At this point Edward Rulloff's motives are absolutely unclear. Many individuals turn to criminal acts when there appear to be no other options for them. Rulloff, on the other hand, was an intelligent man who possessed many talents. His knowledge and use of the law alone could have provided him with a successful career as a lawyer. He was also once a practicing physician with an understanding of chemistry and pharmaceuticals. Even Rulloff's success as a designer of carpets would have surely offered him some means of legitimately employing himself. And above all else, his mastery and love of language would have made him a perfect professor or teacher for a school or institution where he could have established a new life for himself, free from crime. But this was obviously not the case, for Rulloff once again stood before the court to hear his sentence. He had been apprehended in Dutchess County, New York, for theft, and his trial was held in the city of Poughkeepsie. Rulloff was apparently using an alias at the time, for he was tried and sentenced under the name James H. Kerron.

Sing Sing prison was a harsh place to be incarcerated at the time, for each prisoner occupied a cell that was only seven feet deep and three feet wide, but he settled into his life at Sing Sing with ease and soon became quite popular with the other inmates. Rulloff was known as "Big Jim" at the prison and was looked up to by many of the younger men in his cell block. The prison officials also took a liking to him, describing Rulloff as possessing, "a gentlemanly manner and great knowledge of things." He must have convinced the prison guards that he was wrongfully accused of his crime. The warden of the prison put Rulloff to good use, for it was seldom they received such a high-quality prisoner. Rulloff was given the job of managing the prison cabinet-making shop.

It was in the cabinet shop that he began to befriend one of the inmates, a man by the name of William Dexter, who was also serving time for burglary. Rulloff kept the shop running very efficiently, especially the account books, which were maintained in first rate order. His penmanship was still excellent, as the prison account book records which still survive to this day profess. Rulloff's new acquaintance was from New York City, where he had lived life as a petty criminal for most of his years. Dexter was a rough sort of man with little or no education, and at the time he met Rulloff was approximately twenty-five years old. Why Rulloff befriended Dexter is not known, for the two men could not have been more opposite except for their propensity towards crime.

While at Sing Sing, Rulloff also received regular visits from another man, Albert Jarvis, who five years earlier had helped him to escape from the Ithaca Jail. As time went on Rulloff began to form a close alliance with Jarvis and Dexter. Because of his exceptional behavior and his ability to get along with the prison staff, Rulloff's sentence was reduced to two years and six months, and he was once again a free man. Shortly thereafter, his new associate, Dexter, was also released from prison, and the two ex-convicts, along with Albert Jarvis, moved to New York City. Dexter's mother owned a run-down tenement in Brooklyn, and it was there that the three men stayed for a short time.

During this time Rulloff began to work on what he believed to be a great new theory that described how modern languages were formed. During the latter part of the nineteenth century, the science of philology (the study of the origin of languages) was guided by the notion that all of the modern European languages were derived from one ancient language group which was called Indo-European. Through the discipline of comparative linguistics, modern European languages were grouped into major language families. For example, the English and German languages both derive from a language sub-group called Proto-Germanic. In turn, Proto-Germanic, Latin, Greek, and Sanskrit are all derived from the language family called Indo-European. During Rulloff's lifetime, philologists made this great discovery and believed that the Indo-European Language was the oldest language family. Rulloff, however, believed that all languages in the world derived from one common language; he also believed that Ancient Greek held the key to unlocking its secrets. It was to the development of this theory that Rulloff began to devote his life when he moved to New York City in 1864.

When Rulloff arrived in New York he introduced himself to Mrs. Dexter as Jim Howard. Rulloff had no money to his name and looked to the poor Dexter family to support him until he could find work. The Dexters were very impressed with this learned man, and they all looked up to him as someone they could trust.

It was not long after Rulloff, Jarvis, and Dexter came to New York that the three men returned to their life of crime in a most menial manner. Edward Crapsey, one of Rulloff's earlier biographers, described the three men as the "Trinity of Crime" during this time. At first the gang stole potatoes from nearby fields and coal from coal yards to support themselves. What little money they collected from these paltry crimes was immediately seized by Rulloff, for he was the undisputed leader of the group, for whom Jarvis and Dexter would do anything. Rulloff had convinced the two men that he was on the verge of discovering a great new theory of language which would make them all rich.

It is probable that Rulloff directed the criminal activities but rarely participated in them. Evidence of Rulloff's lack of active involvement in the trio's criminal practices was revealed when William Dexter was once again arrested for robbery and sentenced to serve sixty days in the Kings County Penitentiary. Jarvis managed to evade capture, and Rulloff was most likely at work in the Dexter home. This was during the later part of 1864, when Rulloff now had control over his two associates.

Shortly after Dexter's arrest, Rulloff persuaded Mrs. Dexter to put her tenement house up as collateral for a loan of $500, in order to use the money to free her son from jail. He convinced Mrs. Dexter that the best way to handle the transaction was by giving him the power of attorney over her property so he could obtain the loan. Whether it was the result of her own naivety or Rulloff's persuasive personality, she consented, and soon Rulloff was $500 richer. He never used the money to free William Dexter, however, but instead invested it in the development of a new method of coloring photographs. His coloring method failed, but his new position as power of attorney over the Dexter house provided him with a small income. The Dexter house had two upstairs apartments which were rented out, and now Rulloff was in charge of collecting the rent every month. He pooled all of his income, both the money collected by selling the stolen goods Dexter and Jarvis appropriated and the rent money. Then he paid out cash to Jarvis and the Dexters, undoubtedly keeping most of the money for himself.

Rulloff's influence over others' lives culminated when William Dexter was once again released from prison. He convinced both William and his brother John to enlist in the Army. The American Civil War was in its third year and the Union Army needed men to fight. In order to entice men to enlist, the army offered signing bonuses in cash. Amazingly, Rulloff collected both of the Dexter's enlistment incentives and sent the two men off to war. This act once again illustrates the amazing power of persuasion that Rulloff possessed. While the Dexters were off fighting in the war, Rulloff and Jarvis moved out of Mrs. Dexter's home in Brooklyn and into two rooms located in a house on Delancy Street in Manhattan.

The two men lived quietly there; however, their neighbors noticed that occasionally Rulloff and Jarvis would be gone for a few days at a time. Upon their return, the two men always had money. William Dexter returned from his one year commitment to the army and rejoined his two friends in Manhattan. Dexter must not have felt any ill feelings towards Rulloff, who still continued to collect the rent from his mother's tenants and had undoubtedly spent all of his enlistment money.

It wasn't long after Dexter's return that Rulloff and his gang robbed a silk manufacturer on the night of February 14, 1866. The building was located on 35th Street between Eighth and Ninth Avenues in Manhattan. A night watchman by the name of Philip Kraemer was on duty that night on the second floor of the building. The next morning he was found beaten to death, and $2,000 worth of silk cloth was missing. An eyewitness near the building during the time of the theft claimed to see three men fleeing the area, one of whom fit the description of Albert Jarvis. No one was ever convicted of the crime, but the circumstances which surround it certainly point to the work of Rulloff and his men.

Rulloff must have made a good connection for fencing stolen silk cloth, for many of the robberies that his gang carried out involved the theft of textiles. He may have been linked with Frederika "Mother" Mandelbaum, a German immigrant who operated New York City's largest fencing operation at the time. Mandelbaum had managed to build an empire fencing stolen property out of a three story building located on the lower east side of Manhattan. Rulloff could have easily formed an association with Mandelbaum, conversing with her in her native language of German. It was also rumored that Mandelbaum ran a school for would-be thieves in her building. She purportedly trained girls and boys in the art of pickpocketing and older thieves in methods of bank robbery and safe cracking.

Rulloff's possible dealings with Mother Mandlebaum may have induced him to travel eighty-five miles north to Monticello, New York. Sometime in 1868, he arrived there and deposited $200 in the National Bank of Sullivan County. Rulloff rented a room at a local inn and visited the bank often to withdraw small amounts of money, all the while examining the bank, looking for its vulnerabilities. After a few days he took a room at a boarding house where a teller who worked at the bank, George Bennet, resided. Rulloff attempted to befriend Mr. Bennet with his strong persuasive nature. Suspicions must have been raised at the bank by Mr. Bennet, for Rulloff suddenly left town without bothering to withdraw the remaining amount of money he had deposited there. It seems that he had been casing the bank intent on robbing it, but abandoned his plan at the last minute. Why he chose that particular bank is unknown, and why he chose to work without his gang members is also unclear. It could be that his two partners were off on another illegal pursuit.

By 1869 Rulloff's criminal activities must have been quite lucrative, for it was in that year that he moved into comfortable new lodgings in a house located on Third Avenue in Manhattan owned by a man named Conrad Jakob. Rulloff shared his residence with Jarvis and possessed enough cash to devote almost all of his time to working on his theory of language development. Rulloff was now living under the assumed name of Edward Leurio, and he introduced himself to his landlord as a philologist. Mr. Jakob was impressed with his new tenant, for it was indeed a pleasure to rent rooms to such a knowledgeable scholar. Rulloff brought with him his small library and set out to complete what he was now calling his life's work, his thesis titled "Method in the Formation of Language." During this period Rulloff assumed the role of a tireless scholar who was wholly immersed in his intellectual pursuits. There is no doubt that while he was sitting at his desk writing, or studying at one of New York City's great libraries, his accomplices were out stealing to support their master.

It had taken nearly twenty-five years, but Rulloff was once again assuming the role of a highly regarded citizen. Just like he had done when he first arrived in Ithaca, Rulloff was well on his way to becoming a prominent, respected man in Manhattan. The daughter of his landlord often visited his room and listened to the knowledgeable scholar speak. Rulloff also instructed Albert Jarvis in the study of language while they resided on Third Avenue. As time went on he slowly became part of New York's intellectual elite, as word began to spread about his work on a grand theory of languages that would surely revolutionize the philological world. His work was becoming so well-known that in June of 1869, he was invited to speak at a meeting of the Ethnological Society. The Ethnological Society was established in 1842 to foster the study of all aspects of anthropology and the human race. Rulloff arrived at the home of a Dr. Thompson to deliver his lecture to the society's members. Portions of the lecture he gave that night were recorded in a letter written later by Rulloff:

> From the four and twenty letters of an ordinary alphabet, without some special method, such elegant, copious, and euphonious languages as are now in use cannot possibly be formed. At a very remote period the wants of advancing civilization begetting the necessity for such a language, a corresponding method was devised. That method was in the highest degree elegant, philosophical, and artistic. Admitting of numerous applications, and being the only truly philosophic method of which the subject is susceptible, all the leading languages of the human race have since been formed upon it; as the ancient Greek, Latin, [Sanskrit], Hebrew, Arabic, Celtic, German, French, English, etc., etc. The knowledge of the method was for a long time preserved as a secret. It was peculiarly in possession of the priests. It was known only to the initiated, and never taught to the people at large. Unless

still preserved in some secret order, it is now entirely unknown. My manuscript is probably the only work in existence which contains anything like a connected statement of its leading principles. The knowledge of these principles is of the utmost importance to the cause of education, entirely changing the character of philological study as a means of mental discipline. In languages formed upon this plan, words are not merely arbitrary signs. They are signs, each of which is specifically and appropriately significant. Their significance depends upon certain artistic relations, everywhere pervading their structure. The possibility of such a structure depends upon the roots susceptible to change, without loss of identity. Such roots and the mode of their manipulation are certainly unknown to the modern philologist. [Franz] Bopp and others merely observe the presence of similar forms in different languages, or merely trace the course of such forms from one language to another. They do not show their origin in any way. By the knowledge of these roots the very origin of particular words is rendered as perfectly plain and familiar as if we had made them ourselves...When mature consideration has convinced that the etymology of these words is precisely as here stated, and that we do in this way attain to the very origin even of such words as are here given, the mystery of the formation of language is at once and forever dispelled. And when it is realized that these same words are on every hand connected with others by artistic relations distinctly assignable, and that these relations are everywhere in harmony with logical relations in the world around us, profound admiration is felt for the union of philosophical propriety and artistic elegance; philological study is placed in a new light; and restored art is seen to be capable, now, as in days gone by, of exciting the deepest interest even in the youthful mind, and hence, of sub serving the highest purposes in the cause of education.

At the conclusion of his lecture, Rulloff stepped down from the podium and began to distribute a leaflet throughout the assembly of scholars:

GREAT DISCOVERY!!!
METHOD IN THE FORMATION OF LANGUAGE!

The ancient Greek restored. The mystery of the modern languages explained. 5,000 examples.

Taken indiscriminately from the Greek, Latin, German, French and English Languages, their very formation rendered as perfectly plain and familiar as if we had made them ourselves!

Manuscript for sale. Price $500,000.

This manuscript is one of peculiar interest, disclosing a beautiful and unsuspecting method in languages spoken and read by millions of our race. It manipulates the formations of the ancient Greek as things of yesterday; shows the mode of formation of the Latin, German, French, English, and other languages; and ushers in the day when it will no longer be necessary to teach in philology what cannot be thoroughly explained. Its possession is of the utmost importance to the cause of education. There is no other such manuscript in existence.

This manuscript will be formally brought to the notice of the Philological Convention, to meet at Poughkeepsie on the 27th of July, for such action or such recommendation as that body may incline to adopt.

Its present possessor cannot afford to donate it to the public. It has cost him so dearly that the pleasure of producing it must be damped by the necessity of offering it for sale. Communications in regard to it may be addressed, E. Leurio, Box 41 Amity Street Post Office, New York.

The scholars of the Ethnological Society must have been surprised at the costly sum of $500,000 which Rulloff was asking for the publication of his theory. Members of the society present that night remembered Rulloff's presentation vividly, recalling that when "Mr. Leurio spoke of his theory it was with maniacal enthusiasm." Although his theory was of a very original nature, and Rulloff certainly possessed a very great knowledge of philological principles and of language in general, the theory was too far removed from the popular beliefs of the time. Rulloff most assuredly insulted the few philologists who attended the meeting by discrediting their modern theories. In his lecture he specifically mentions Franz Bopp, who was the world's most highly regarded comparative linguist at the time. For him to regard Bopp as "merely observing the presence of similar forms from one language or another..." and "not showing the origin [of language] in any way..." must have been insulting to many linguists in attendance. Nevertheless, Rulloff was praised by the society for his scholarly pursuits, and wished the best of luck when he was to attend the Philological Convention.

Rulloff left the meeting that evening and rode down Sixth Avenue with a newspaper reporter who had listened to his lecture. Rulloff hoped that the newspaper might publish some of his work, but the reporter refused, stating that it was not yet accepted by the philological community. The reporter told Rulloff that if he received the endorsement from the American Philological Society, then he might change his mind. Rulloff returned to his room on Third Avenue and continued his work.

It is interesting to observe how Rulloff lived during this period. He immersed himself into the life of an academic who was received by the scholarly circles of New York City. This in itself reveals that Rulloff was well regarded by his contemporaries; however, at the same time, this "scholar" was also the mastermind of one of New York's most elusive criminal gangs. Rulloff supported his academic pursuits almost exclusively by the criminal acts performed by his two hooligans, Jarvis and Dexter. The only other income that Rulloff had at the time was from his rent collections in Brooklyn, which he legally appropriated from Mrs. Dexter.

It is possible to draw some similarities between the life of Edward Rulloff during this time and that of the fictional character of Professor Moriarty created by Sir Arthur Conan Doyle. Professor Moriarty was the criminal mastermind and nemesis of the great detective, Sherlock Holmes. Moriarty, also known as the "Napoleon of Crime," directed a crime syndicate in London while also being a highly regarded scholar of mathematics and astronomy. Although many Sherlock Homes enthusiasts believe the character of Moriarty was based on Adam Worth, a real-life pickpocket and thief, Rulloff is a much better model for the fictional villain. Unlike

Worth, both Moriarty and Rulloff were extremely intelligent and shared a love for scholarly pursuits. They both published monographs on their work, and of course both directed criminal activities. It is also interesting to note that even the physical characteristics of these two men were very similar. Doyle described Professor Moriarty as possessing a very large head which was tilted at a strange angle. This depicts Rulloff's attributes perfectly. Although it cannot be proven, it is certainly plausible that Sir Arthur Conan Doyle was aware of Rulloff's life story after it was revealed in the early 1870s. Regardless of the coincidence between Professor Moriarty and Rulloff, the latter was certainly living a double life that few people could have imagined in nineteenth century New York City.

Rulloff's life at this time was described later by his former landlady, Mrs. Jakob, who portrayed him as a perfect gentleman who studied night and day when he was in his rooms. He amassed a large library while living on Third Avenue, which contained books on subjects ranging from language to the natural sciences. Rulloff was also rather popular with the neighborhood children whom he often talked with and gave pennies to.

In July of 1869, Rulloff was looking forward to traveling to Poughkeepsie, New York, where he was going to attend the First Annual Convention of the American Philological Association. He realized that he needed their endorsement to have his theory of language formation accepted. The convention began on July 29 and in attendance were all of the prominent American philologists of the time. Rulloff appealed to the convention to allow him to present his theory of the formation of modern languages. A motion was passed by the convention president to appoint Dr. Raymond and Professor Hackness to form a committee to review Rulloff's manuscript and report on its merit to the advancement of philological investigation. Rulloff also tried to personally approach every scholar attending the convention and lobby for the support of his work.

The result of the Philological Convention's committee report was unfavorable, however, and they decided not to endorse Rulloff's thesis. One of the principle reasons that the Philological Association turned against Rulloff was his claim that all languages were related and shared a common origin. The implication of a common language being shared by all was that all human beings must also have shared a common heritage. European scholars especially took offense to this, because it suggested that all humans were related. This ran counter to Western thought at the time, for it was believed that the European race was superior to all others.

This is part of the reason that nineteenth century philologists believed that the Indo-European language family was not related to others like the Afro-Asiatic or Niger Kordofanian language families which encompassed many African and Middle Eastern languages. This race superiority notion was very prevalent in the nineteenth century and governed many academic theories.

Rulloff's "Method in the Formation of Language" was unusual, especially in its claim that some secret sect or organization of priests methodically designed roots to be applied to language. However, his theory was ahead of its time in one respect: the notion that modern languages may have been derived from one common source. Today, many historic linguists, anthropologists, and geneticists are trying to substantiate the theory of a common origin of human languages. This theory is called scientific monogenesis, or "The Mother Tongue Theory," which relies on genetics, anthropology, and historic linguistics to trace back the origin of humans and human language to the African continent somewhere around 150,000 years ago. Unfortunately it took a person like Rulloff to look beyond race to find common roots shared by all human beings. This alone was a great accomplishment for a nineteenth century scholar.

The cool reception given to Rulloff's language theories by the American Philological Association surely must have angered the frustrated scholar; nevertheless, he continued to compile the 5,000 examples he promised which would substantiate his theory. Not long after the Philological Convention in late 1869, Rulloff traveled to Cortland, New York, to attend to some urgent business. William Dexter was once again arrested, this time in Cortland, and Rulloff, using the name James Dalton, appeared as his lawyer. This fact was recalled by Sheriff Brown, who remembered that Mr. Dalton (Rulloff) gave Dexter, who was using the alias William Davenport, some money to purchase books to read while awaiting trial. The sheriff's son, Charles Brown, purchased the books for Dexter. Rulloff succeeded in having the charges against his accomplice dropped, and the two men returned to New York City.

Dexter's arrest is yet another example of how Rulloff continued to manage his criminal activities while living in New York City. Jarvis and Dexter were undoubtedly sent off on specific criminal missions dictated by their master. They would then return to New York City where Rulloff would resell the stolen goods and divide the profits. Occasionally, Rulloff would have to assume a new identity and go off and retrieve one of his gang members from jail if they had been apprehended. The town of Cortland, where Dexter had been caught, was located only about twenty miles northeast of Ithaca. At around that same time, a robbery occurred in Ithaca that may have also been the work of Rulloff's gang.

Once again it seemed the town of Ithaca was to be affected by Rulloff's wrongdoings. Many of the townspeople had gathered to attend the dedication of one of the buildings recently constructed for the new Cornell University, which was located on a hill overlooking the town. While this ceremony was going on, Wilgus' Store was robbed of many of its silk fabrics. Although the case was never solved, the nature of the crime certainly fits Rulloff's modus operandi. It was also revealed later that Albert Jarvis was known to have stayed at the Ithaca Hotel at the time and was seen mingling through the crowd at the Cornell ceremony. It seems likely that his reason for being in Ithaca was to help execute one of Rulloff's criminal plans, and not to celebrate the opening of a new building on the Cornell campus or visit with his family.

Although many of the "Trinity of Crime's" activities were committed without Rulloff being present, this was not the case when the three men traveled to Binghamton, New York, in the summer of 1870. The purpose of their visit to this small city was to investigate the possibility of robbing a store that was currently being renovated. The store was located near the Chenango River, and an addition was being built on the building's back end which faced the river. The store was run by the Halbert brothers, who sold dry goods and also had a fine stock of silks.

On the night of August 12, 1870, at approximately two o'clock in the morning, Rulloff, Dexter, and Jarvis stealthily crept along the banks of the Chenango River. Their objective was the addition to Halbert's store which was still under construction. The men approached a temporary door on the addition that faced the river. Jarvis and Dexter succeeded in drilling three holes in the door, using them to release the three bolts which held the door in place. With the door open, the three men silently entered the structure. They carried with them some tools and a lamp which was fixed to shine very dim light. The trio also wore masks made from canvas, and Rulloff carried a revolver. They made their way through the construction area and arrived at a stairway that led to the main floor of the store. Rulloff had to pause to remove his Oxford shoes, which were making too much noise as they ascended the stairs. His accomplices, obviously more used to the art of robbery, were wearing moccasins which made their movements much more silent. The two thieves and their scholarly leader cautiously climbed to the top of the stairway and saw that two men were sleeping on cots in the middle of the room. The men were Gilbert Burrows and Frederick Mirrick, both store clerks who were there to guard the place while it was under construction. The three thieves cautiously approached the two sleeping clerks, intent on tying them up before they awoke.

As the men slowly neared the cots, the two clerks suddenly woke up and confronted the three men. Jarvis, Dexter, and Rulloff became startled and turned to run for the stairs. Mirrick reached for a pistol and aimed it at the fleeing men; his pistol misfired twice. Burrows managed to grab Dexter and hit him over the head with an iron box opener which caused him to drop to the ground. Mirrick, abandoning his faulty revolver, began to throw wooden stool tops at Jarvis as he fled. Seeing that one of the burglars was down, Mirrick helped Burrows seize Dexter, who began to scream for help. Rulloff and Jarvis dashed down the stairs to escape, but the two men turned and went back up upon hearing Dexter's plea for help. When Rulloff, who was wearing a mask to conceal his face, arrived near the top of the stairs, he came face to face with Burrows. Rulloff stopped, pointed his revolver, and fired three shots at Burrows. All of the bullets missed their mark, but one struck the railing on the stairs and sent wood splinters flying into Burrows' face. Thinking that he had been shot, Burrows fell to the floor. Rulloff walked quickly past Burrows and approached Mirrick, who had Dexter pinned down. Rulloff put his hand on the back of Mirrick's neck and his pistol barrel directly at the back of his head and fired. The bullet ripped into Mirrick's brain, and the clerk fell to the floor. Rulloff then helped Dexter up, and the three men fled the building the same way they came in. Shortly after the Rulloff gang fled, Burrows got up from the floor and ran towards the front door. He opened it and began yelling out into the street that a murder had just occurred. The sleeping city was soon awakened to the tragic news of the robbery.

Rulloff and his accomplices ran down towards the river, where he ordered them to split up and meet in Batavia in a few days. Prior to their arrival in Binghamton, Rulloff had purchased three railroad tickets to Batavia which each of the men had in their pockets. Rulloff bid his men good luck and disappeared into the darkness. Jarvis was left to tend to the wounded Dexter, who was suffering from the blow to the head he received back in the store. Jarvis, most likely scared and confused, made a fateful decision, knowing that the town was waking up and would soon be searching the area. He decided to try to cross the Chenango River and flee into the countryside. It is surmised that Dexter and Jarvis began to ford the river, which was at first remarkably shallow. The cold water moved swiftly as Jarvis and Dexter struggled across toward the center of its dark waters. Suddenly, the two men found themselves plunging into a deep portion of the river which was over their heads, and they were immediately dragged under. The ailing Dexter began to struggle and grabbed onto Jarvis for help. Eventually the two men were overcome by the river and drowned.

Rulloff, not knowing the fate of his accomplices, moved quietly along the banks of the river and headed south into the meadows and forests which surrounded the city. While the burglars attempted their escape, the city of Binghamton was awakened with excitement. James Flynn, the chief of the Binghamton Police, arrived on the scene quickly because he was staying at the hotel across the street. A doctor was immediately summoned to help the wounded Mirrick. Chief Flynn called for volunteers to set up a cordon of pickets to encircle the city and prevent the perpetrators from leaving the area. The unfortunate store clerk, Frederick Mirrick, died an hour later from his gunshot wound. He was only nineteen years old.

As the sun rose in the city, the investigation to identify the murderers was underway. As the police searched the store in the daylight, they discovered a number of items left behind by the burglars. Among these were a pair of leather Oxford shoes which had been left at the bottom of the stairs. The left shoe had a remarkable feature, for there was a large indentation where the big toe would have been. The discovery of Rulloff's shoes suggested that one of the burglars was missing his left big toe. (Rulloff's, of course had been amputated fourteen years earlier.) Other items left behind by the burglars included a canvas mask and some tools.

The police carefully traced the footprints of the burglars from the rear door of the store's new addition. Two sets of tracks left behind were made by men wearing moccasins. The police followed these until they reached the river. The other set of tracks leading from the store were made by a person in his stocking feet. These were followed until they disappeared into the high grass along the banks of the river. The only clue to the identity of the perpetrators of one of Binghamton's worst crimes was the curious pair of shoes that were left behind at the scene. All that the police could hope for now was the apprehension of the three men as they attempted to flee the area.

Two nights after the break-in, a pair of volunteers who were helping to cordon off the area around Binghamton spied a man walking towards them on the railroad tracks. They had been stationed at the Erie Railroad bridge ten miles south of the city. The volunteers approached the man and inquired why he was walking alone at midnight. The man, who was Edward Rulloff, replied that he was on the train to New York City and was removed because of his lack of money to pay the fare. As the men continued their inquiry, a fast-moving freight train approached. Just as the train was about to pass them, Rulloff quickly ran in front of it to the other side of the railroad tracks and escaped from the two sentries. When the train had finally passed, Rulloff was gone.

The two men began to search the area near the railroad bridge. In a home nearby, a man by the name of Chauncy Livingston was awakened by the sound of the freight train. After it had passed, he heard some odd noises, grabbed his gun, and went out onto his back porch. While he stood outside in the darkness, he heard the sounds of the sentries searching in the woods, but not knowing who they were, he remained silent and listened. As he gazed out into the night, he noticed that the door to his outhouse was open. This was not usually the case, so he cautiously approached and peered inside with his revolver in hand. He found a man crouching in the corner; it was Edward Rulloff. Livingston pulled the man out of the shack and inquired who he was and why he was hiding. Rulloff told the same story that he told the sentries, that he had been ejected from the train to New York for lack of train fare. Livingston, not believing his story, called out to the men in the woods who quickly arrived and told him about the situation. Rulloff was then escorted back into Binghamton at gunpoint.

Rulloff was brought before Chief Flynn early the next morning. The chief asked him who he was and why he had tried to run. Rulloff introduced himself as George Williams and related the story that he told to the men who brought him in. Rulloff possessed a haughty attitude, declaring that he was a lawyer from Brooklyn and could not be held for lack of sufficient charges. Then, in a strange twist of irony, Judge Balcom walked into the chief's office. Balcom was the judge who had presided over the case of the murder of Rulloff's daughter over ten years earlier in Tioga County. The judge happened to be in the Binghamton area and had come to the chief's office to learn about the recent crime. Balcom immediately recognized the accused and informed the men in the room that the man they were questioning was Edward H. Rulloff, who murdered his wife and daughter in Lansing and served ten years in prison for abduction. Rulloff, who must have been stunned by the unfortunate timing of Judge Balcom's visit, responded in a very cool manner. He said that it was true that he was Edward Rulloff and that he gave a false name, because after being in the area and hearing of the tragedy, he felt it better to hide his identity for fear of being wrongfully accused of the crime. Rulloff continued to tell the men that he was just a victim of circumstance.

As the chief and the judge were deciding what to do about Rulloff, they were notified that two bodies had been discovered floating in the Chenango River. The two men were believed to be part of the threesome who attempted to rob Halbert's store. The men decided to take Rulloff along with them when they went to inspect the bodies in the basement of the police station. The Chief of Police asked Rulloff if he knew the men who were laid out on the table. This must have been a difficult moment for Rulloff, for this was the first time he had learned of the fate of his two accomplices; however, he examined the two bodies with indifference and declared that he never saw them before in his life.

After some more consideration, and given the lack of evidence, Chief Flynn and Judge Balcom apologized to Rulloff for detaining him. The three men all shook hands; Rulloff bid the men good day and left the office, once again a free man. Amazingly, he had succeeded in talking his way out of what seemed to be a dire situation. Another incredible triumph had just been accomplished by Rulloff, for now he could add the title of successful actor to his life achievements. Francis Finch, one of Rulloff's lawyers, tried to capture Rulloff's performance in the Binghamton Police Office in this portion of a poem that he wrote about his former client:

> To brand me cobbler! Thief ingrained. A scholar learned,
> physician trained. Teacher versed in languages, a chemist
> taught to trace and seize the secrets of all elements! And
> yet a thief!

After Rulloff left, the police brought Gilbert Burrows in to identify the bodies. Although bloated and decayed after being in the river for two days, Burrows positively identified the men as two of the three who had perpetrated the crime. The contents found in their pockets also helped to connect them to the robbery, for Jarvis still had the drill bits in his pocket that fit the holes which had been drilled into the rear door of the store. Each man was also carrying a railroad ticket for a one way trip to Batavia, New York. Chief Flynn and Judge Balcom together began to assess the facts that they knew about the recent tragedy at Halbert's store. Flynn told Balcom that the only evidence they had to identify the third person involved in the crime was the pair of shoes that had been left behind. Balcom asked what was so significant about the shoes. The chief informed him that the left shoe was unique in that it had a depression near the big toe, suggesting that the person who owned the shoes was missing his left big toe. Balcom must have turned white at this revelation, for he rose from his chair and exclaimed to Chief Flynn that Edward Rulloff was missing his left toe as a result of frostbite. The two men immediately dashed out of the office and ordered that Rulloff be apprehended at once. This time it was not as difficult to find Rulloff, for he now assumed he was a free man and had taken his time leaving the area.

Rulloff was confronted by a deputy by the name of Brown about four miles outside of Binghamton. He told Rulloff that the authorities had decided to detain him once again. Rulloff asked why, and Brown replied by asking Rulloff to remove his left boot and sock. Rulloff complied with the order and revealed his deformed foot. He was then returned to Binghamton and arrested for the crimes that took place at Halbert's store. Shortly after his arrest, Rulloff was forced to try on the shoes that were left in the store the night of the attack. They fit perfectly, but Rulloff argued that he always wore boots, and the ones he was found in had no indentation in the toe. It was revealed that a wad of cotton had been stuffed into the boot to prevent an indentation from forming. It appeared that Edward Rulloff was running out of excuses. He must have cursed his bad luck, for he was extremely close to escaping punishment for the failed burglary and murder. It seemed that fate had intervened, and his past was now coming back to haunt him. If it wasn't for Judge Balcom's coincidental visit to the Binghamton Police Department, Rulloff would have certainly returned to New York City and may have never been connected to the crime.

MY WORK IS DONE

ecause of Rulloff's reputation as a shrewd legal manipulator, Binghamton's District Attorney, Peter Hopkins, traveled to New York City to gather as much evidence as he could to strongly support his case against Rulloff. One of the clues that lead him there was the identification of William Dexter as one of the drowned perpetrators. Hopkins learned that Dexter, who had been recently released from jail in Cortland, had lived in New York City.

When Hopkins arrived in New York, he gained the assistance of Captain Hedden and Detective Reilly of the New York City Police Department. The men tracked down Dexter's home in Brooklyn and questioned the tenants who lived upstairs. Hopkins showed them a picture of Rulloff and learned that he had been living under the assumed identity of E. C. Howard, and that he had been in charge of collecting the rent for the Dexter family apartment building. One of the people who identified Rulloff told the police that Mr. Howard was a shrewd lawyer who managed to get William Dexter out of trouble whenever he had run-ins with the law.

District Attorney Hopkins had also brought along a set of keys which had been found in Rulloff's possession when he was arrested in Binghamton. The keys were traced to the apartment he rented from the Jakob family at 170 Third Avenue. When the three investigators arrived at the house, the Jakob family was shocked to hear the reason the police were searching Rulloff's rooms. They couldn't believe their resident scholar, whom they knew as Mr. Edward Leurio, could be responsible for such a horrendous crime. It didn't take long for the police to discover burglary tools in the apartment, along with an incriminating newspaper. When Rulloff was apprehended near the railroad bridge outside of Binghamton, a carpet bag had also been discovered lying near the tracks. When Rulloff was detained he denied that the bag was his. In it were some burglary tools and a newspaper clipping from a *New York Times* article describing the U. S. government's relations with Persia. The newspaper that the article was cut from was discovered on Rulloff's desk in New York City.

With enough evidence in hand to connect Rulloff with Dexter and the Binghamton murder, District Attorney Hopkins returned home. Upon his arrival he learned that the other dead man found in the river had been identified as Albert Jarvis. Jarvis' mother was called to Binghamton to verify the identity of her son. Afterwards, Mrs. Jarvis was also asked to identify Rulloff. Surprisingly, she told the police that she had never seen him before. This was unexpected considering that her husband had once been in charge of the jail in which Rulloff was held captive and from which he eventually escaped. One of Rulloff's earlier biographers, Samuel Halliday, believed that this lie by Mrs. Jarvis suggests she might have been involved with Rulloff's "Trinity of Crime."

With all of the evidence gathered, Rulloff's trial began on January 5, 1871, in the city of Binghamton, New York. The excitement that the trial was causing in the region was reported by the *New York Times*:

> The great sensation of the populous and prosperous region of which Binghamton is the center has become intensified, but in no degree satisfied, by the events of the day. The prisoner, Edward H. Rulloff, charged with the double crime of burglary and murder, has emerged from obscurity where he has hidden for the past four months, and hundreds have eagerly sought to catch even a passing glance of him as he walked over the few rods of ground between the prison and the Court-room. During the seven hours of monotonous labor consumed in the task [of jury selection], the audience, largely composed of ladies, waited with unwearied patience for the more interesting aspects of the case.

Rulloff's counsel was composed of Mr. George Becker and Mr. Charles Beale, and the trial was presided over by Judge Hogeboom. The prosecution opened its case by presenting the facts which established a link between Rulloff and the two drowned men. They began by tracing Rulloff's involvement with Albert Jarvis all the way back to the time when he was housed in the Ithaca Jail. As Rulloff listened he appeared nervous, grabbed the arm of his defense lawyer, and whispered something in his ear. Soon after, the defense objected to the prosecution's allusion to Rulloff's past crimes; however, the judge overruled the objection on the grounds that it helped to establish Rulloff's relationship with Jarvis, and therefore the crime. The prosecution then presented the physical evidence they had gathered which implicated Rulloff in the robbery, the most crucial of which were the shoes with the indented toe that were discovered at the crime scene. District Attorney Hopkins concluded his statements by telling the jury how Rulloff escaped the indictment of murder for the deaths of his wife and child nearly ten years earlier on the basis that no body was ever found. Hopkins turned to Rulloff and said, "In this case there will be no reversal of your verdict because the body of the crime is wanting." The prosecution's presentation lasted fifty-four minutes, and the court adjourned until the following day when the witnesses would be presented.

The next day in court brought profound changes to the defense's strategy, for Rulloff decided he would cross-examine the first prosecution witness, Gilbert Burrows, the store clerk who was present the night of the botched robbery and was the only surviving eyewitness to the crime. Rulloff asked Burrows if there was sufficient light in the building to be able to accurately identify the man who shot and killed the other clerk, Frederick Mirrick. Burrows replied that there was. Rulloff demanded that the witness testify exactly how much light there was that night. Burrows replied, "Well, I can't say, you know, how much light there was!" His reply caused the crowded courtroom to erupt with laughter, which was immediately ceased by the Judge. Rulloff showed no signs of emotion as he sat down.

The next group of witnesses called by the prosecution helped piece together Rulloff's life while he resided in New York City and his link to Jarvis and Dexter. Rulloff continued to object that the testimonies of these witnesses were extremely circumstantial at best. The prosecution also produced a photograph of the two drowned men, Jarvis and Dexter, as evidence to substantiate their identities. This was one of the first uses of photographic evidence in a criminal case in the United States. Rulloff argued about its admissibility, asking how it could be proven that a photograph produced an exact likeness of an individual. The court ruled that a photograph can be used at trial as a means of identification. Once again, Rulloff was involved in another monumental American legal decision; however, this time it was not in his favor.

The prosecution rested its case after Dr. N. S. Burr testified that he had examined the feet of the two drowned men and found that neither of them was missing a toe. This was the most damaging testimony in the case, for Rulloff's left foot with its missing big toe fit the shoes that were left behind at the crime scene perfectly. It was impossible for Rulloff to talk his way out of that fact, and he didn't even bother to cross examine the witness. The prosecution then rested its case.

The defense conducted its case by arguing two points. The first was the fact that only circumstantial evidence connected Rulloff with the drowned men thought to be two of the three burglars, even though Rulloff's shoes were found at the scene. The second point was that the death of Mirrick was only the result of an attempt to thwart the unnecessary violence being inflicted upon Dexter by the two store clerks as they tried to subdue him. The defense argued that although his death was unfortunate, it should be regarded as manslaughter and not first degree murder. The defense also tried to discredit the testimonies of some of the prosecution's witnesses, especially that of Burrows, the eyewitness who claimed Rulloff shot and killed Mirrick. The defense then rested its case.

The next day, after some guidance to the jury from the Attorney General and Judge Hogeboom, the jury left the courtroom to deliberate. A little over four hours later the verdict was decided: Edward Rulloff was found guilty of murder in the first degree. In response to the defense's arguments, the court handed down the following ruling concerning the uncertainty regarding which of the three men fired the fatal shot.

> If the homicide was committed by one of several persons in the prosecution of an unlawful purpose or common design in which the combining parties had united, and for the effecting whereof they had assembled, all were liable to answer criminality for the act; and if the homicide was murder, all were guilty of murder, assuming that it was within the common purpose.

The court then addressed Rulloff's argument that the death of Mirrick was the result of his own unnecessary use of violence towards the burglars, and therefore should be regarded as manslaughter:

> One who is opposing and endeavoring to prevent the commission of a felony by others may properly use all necessary force for that purpose. Although the use of wanton violence and the infliction of unnecessary injury to the person of the criminal is not permitted, yet the law will not be astute in searching for such line of demarcation in this respect as will take the innocent citizen whose property and life are in danger from its protection and place his life at the mercy of the felon.

The decision of the jury was affirmed by the court, and the following day Rulloff was sentenced to be executed. He showed no outward emotion as his sentence was handed down, which was not surprising for a man who had been sentenced to death twice already in his life. Rulloff, upon returning to prison to await his execution, immediately began to work on his appeal. His legal angle this time relied on something wholly unique, his own study of philology. In another unprecedented move, Rulloff compiled a petition to be sent directly to Governor John T. Hoffman. In his extensive request, Rulloff addressed two points. The first point he stressed, in great length, was the illegality of his murder conviction. He outlined the similar arguments that were the basis of his defense during his trial. However, it was his second point in the petition which presented a unique appeal. Referring to himself in the third person, Rulloff stated:

> He has recently made as to all cultivated language an important discovery; he has at his disposal neither the time or the means necessary to perpetuate that discovery; and whatever may be his own fate, the discovery should on no account be permitted to perish, or to pass again from the knowledge of our race. He has been for many years more or less engaged in philological research. His investigations have lead to the discovery of a beautiful method of cultivated language. Till now this method has been in modern times entirely unknown. It so far transcends in elegance and in art all that has been hitherto regarded as possible in language, that to minds unprepared, its

principles are nearly incomprehensible, and the mere statement of them often causes your petitioner to be regarded as insane. That, nevertheless, the discovery is real, and its preservation of the utmost importance.

In itself, it is of infinite interest, as disclosing the most curious chapter of the intellectual history of our race. In its bearing upon the cause of education, it is of equal importance, as accounting thoroughly for the origin for all cultivated languages, as showing their formation to be in the highest degree artistic, and as tracing between different and corresponding words in all cultivated languages, relations the most curious, yet perfectly methodical.

It rests upon philosophical principles. It applies equally to the ancient Greek, Latin, Hebrew, [Sanskrit], Arabic, Celtic, French, German, English, and other languages. It shows that they are all formations upon precisely the same plan. It enables us to trace in any of them with equal ease the precise origin of the various words. It carries us back to a time in the history of the ancient Greek, when as yet the letter R was unknown. It shows where that letter was obtained and by whom it was brought into Greece. It identifies with various methodical applications of this letter, the most pleasing fiction of ancient mythology; and by furnishing a rational explanation of those fictions, it enhances their interest, and renders them truly instructive...in behalf of the cause of education, and of millions yet unborn, he implores that the sentence of death may not be executed upon him until this has been done...

Rulloff's petition also contained some examples of his language theory and how it was used to trace the origins of modern language. His request was created to prove to the governor that his scholarly achievements were necessary to the advancement of education, and to put him to death at such an important juncture for the advancement of human understanding would be contrary to all that human beings were trying to achieve. His petition did succeed in having the governor look into Rulloff's matter more closely; however, instead of forming a committee to investigate the importance of his language discovery, Governor Hoffman appointed a committee to determine if Rulloff might be insane.

The convicted murderer was not the only one who was petitioning the governor for a stay of execution. Not long after Rulloff was sentenced to be executed, the famous writer and humorist Samuel Langhorne Clemens, better known a Mark Twain, wrote a letter to the editor of the *New York Tribune*, which was published on May 3, 1871. Using his famous wit, Clemens appealed to the authorities to spare Rulloff as a result of his superior intellect, and even offered to produce a person to take Rulloff's place at the hangman's noose:

To the Editor of The Tribune.

> Sir: I believe in capital punishment. I believe that when a murder has been done it should be answered for in blood. I have all my life been taught to feel this way, and the fetters of education are strong. The fact that the death law is rendered almost inoperative by its very severity does not alter my belief in its righteousness....
>
> Feeling as I do, I am not sorry that Rulloff is to be hanged, but I am sincerely sorry that he himself has made it necessary that his vast capabilities for usefulness should be lost to the world. In this, mine and the public's is a common regret. For it is plain that in the person of Rulloff one of the most marvelous intellects that any age has produced is about to be sacrificed, and that, too, while half the mystery of its strange powers is yet a secret. Here is a man who has never entered the doors of a college or a university, and yet, by the sheer might of his innate gifts has made himself such a colossus in abstruse learning that the ablest of our scholars are but pigmies in his presence..... this man is as familiar with the broad domain of philology as common people are with passing events of the day. His memory has such a limitless grasp that he is able to quote sentence after sentence, paragraph after paragraph, and chapter after chapter, from a gnarled and knotty ancient literature that ordinary scholars are capable of achieving a little more than bowing acquaintance with. But his memory is the least of his great endowments....Every

learned man who enters Rulloff's presence leaves them amazed and confounded by his prodigious capabilities and attainments....What miracles this murderer might have wrought, and what luster he might have shed upon this country if he had not put a forfeit upon his life so foolishly! But what if the law could be satisfied, and the gifted criminal still be saved. If a life be offered up on the gallows to atone for the murder Rulloff did, will that suffice? If so, give me the proofs, for, in all earnestness and truth, I aver that in such a case I will instantly bring forward a man who, in the interests of learning and science, will *take Rulloff's crime upon himself, and submit to be hanged in Rulloff's place.* I can, and will do this thing; and I propose to do this matter, and make this offer in good faith. You know me, and know my address.

Samuel Langhorne

Clemens had close ties with the *New York Tribune*, and along with his letter, he sent a personal note to its managing editor. In it he stated that his offer should be taken in jest, and it was written to help drum up public support for commuting Rulloff's sentence to that of life in prison rather than execution.

As Rulloff waited in his cell for the response to his petition, he continued to devote his time to the completion of his language theory. During the trial, his manuscript on the formation of language was used as evidence to connect him to the room he was renting in New York with Dexter and Jarvis. Luckily for Rulloff, the manuscript was returned to him after the trial ended. While awaiting his fate, many people attempted to visit Rulloff in his cell. He refused interviews with most of them, stating that they were only out to darken his name or exploit his situation.

One visitor, however, was granted an interview. This man was Professor R.H. Mather from Amherst College in Massachusetts. Mather had become interested in Rulloff when a colleague presented him with a copy of a criticism that Rulloff had written about Lewis' edition of Plato's *Dialogues*. The monograph had been written when he was in prison at Auburn over twenty years earlier. The paper so impressed Mather that he decided to speak with the condemned man. At first Rulloff refused to talk with

Mather, but when he learned that he was a teacher of the Greek language, he granted him an interview. Rulloff was anxious for Mather to hear about his theory. The two language scholars proceeded to discuss Greek literature; Rulloff was able to recite by memory many passages of the works of Homer, Sophocles, and Socrates. Mather was certainly impressed with Rulloff's knowledge, although he found his theory on the formations of language very strange. Rulloff pleaded with Mather to return with a committee to review his manuscript, emphasizing, "And you know whatever be done must be done quickly." Mather later recalled his impression of the man he visited in the cell that day:

> In person this strange man is about middle height and of robust build and is apparently verging on fifty years of age. In manners he is very urban and natural, and he converses with great faculty and elegance. His voice is mellow and pleasant, and occasionally showed the tones of tenderness. But for all that, I do not believe the man has any tenderness save for language. In looking at him you would be sure that his hatred would be implacable. He is certainly an enigma, and offers in himself a powerful argument against the theory that education is alone sufficient to lead to true manhood.

Mather's interview with Rulloff must have certainly weighed heavily upon him, for he used his experience to illustrate the importance of moral education in our society:

> Here is a profound and appreciative student of all that is beautiful and glorious in classical learning, working for years as a philologist, and with a zeal rarely equaled; and yet all the time living a life of crime as dark and terrible as any criminal in our land. He shows us that true culture and true manhood can only be a development of the moral sense.

On the 10th of May, 1871, Rulloff was busy writing at a small table in his cell when he was greeted by three visitors who had been sent by the governor. They introduced themselves as Doctors Gray and Vanderpool, who were accompanied by their secretary, Mr. Dwight King. Rulloff was told that they had been sent by the governor to examine him and decide on the state of his mental health. This was the first time Rulloff had heard any news relating to the petition that he had sent to the governor in Albany. Upon learning of their intentions, Rulloff told them, "Gentlemen, this is no work of mine. I don't pretend to be either insane or an idiot. I am feeble in body as you may see; but this has not affected my mind. The proposal of the commission is no move of mine." The men were welcomed into Rulloff's cell and they proceeded with the examination. At first they questioned him about his physical condition; he replied that he had not been in the best of health since his stay at Auburn Prison. Next they inquired where he received his education, which of course was the result of his own doing. Then they asked him about his philological studies. Rulloff told the men about his theory pertaining to the formation of language, giving the men a lesson in its workings. Finally they questioned him about his religious beliefs, which revealed much about Rulloff's true inner workings. The following is a transcript from the interview:

Q: Can you account for man's being brought into existence?
A: No it is beyond thought; we can neither conceive how man could have been created, or how he could remain uncreated.
Q: Is the contemplation of God beyond the scope of men?
A: No, for there are men who lead religious lives and spend their time in contemplating God.
Q: Have their studies, their contemplation and their lives realized anything towards their knowledge of God as a creator and governor of the world?
A: No, for they all have different ideas of Him.
Q: Do you believe that such a being exists?
A: I don't know. I ascent to nothing but what is reducible to mathematical precision. I must prove it to my senses. I cannot accept anything not cognizable by the senses.
Q: Would the fact of another existence, and that existence of rewards and punishments for your conduct in this life, make any difference to you in regard to your acts?
A: No, I should do as I intended without the regard to the existence of a God or a devil, a heaven or a hell. I have felt this pride during my whole life.

The men conversed with Rulloff for quite a while and then completed the examination. The results of their interview were presented in a formal report to Governor Hoffman a few days later which concluded, "Your commissioners, therefore in view of the examination, are of the opinion that Edward H. Rulloff is in sound physical health and entirely sane."

Five days following the report of Doctors Vanderpool and Gray, Rulloff was greeted by his attorney, George Becker, who had just received a telegram from Governor Hoffman in response to Rulloff's petition. The telegram stated there would be no respite or commutation of his case, and he was to be executed as planned the next day. Rulloff erupted in a rage and began to spew forth a multitude of curses. He blasted the governor for being dictated by his political ambition and stated that his name, rather than Governor Hoffman's, would be remembered far into the future. Rulloff then returned to his table and continued to work on his manuscript. His behavior did not reflect the fact that he was to die by the hangman's noose in less than twenty-four hours.

Rulloff's last effort was to try and publicize his theory of language formation by publishing a section of his manuscript in the *New York Times*. Fearing that his life story would be grossly exaggerated, he ended his newspaper article with the following statement, "This is to certify that I have never in any way contributed to the preparation of a work to be sold as my life, and such work purporting to be written from information furnished by me, will be fraudulent and untrue."

The morning of his execution, May 18, 1871, a large crowd began to gather around the courthouse in downtown Binghamton. A scaffold had been constructed which held a pulley and rope. On one end of the rope was a noose. On the other end was a large sack which weighed in excess of two hundred pounds. Rulloff was to be hoisted up by his neck to a height of about one foot above the ground by the weight of the sack and hung until dead. His execution was to occur at about eleven thirty that morning, but the crowd arrived early in order to get a good look at the condemned man.

Rulloff was awake in his cell when Sheriff Martin appeared at his door as the time for his execution arrived. He was asked if he would like to see the two priests who were waiting outside. Rulloff did not wish to see the clergyman, but he told the sheriff to make sure that his belongings were delivered to his brother, Ruloff Rulofson. He also instructed him to have his body attended to by his brother after his death. Rulloff then returned to his table and began to straighten things up.

At twenty past eleven he was taken from his cell and brought into a waiting room. As he walked down the corridor he passed his own coffin, which was being stored in the hall until it was needed. He was greeted by his lawyers and Chief Flynn. Rulloff shook hands with his counsel and thanked them for their help. He then told Sheriff Martin to make sure there were no clergy down in the yard waiting for him. Finally Rulloff was lead outside to meet his end. The crowd pushed forward to try to get a glimpse of him as he was led to the rope. Waiting in the courtyard were some of the members of the Schutt family, who came to see the death of the man who stole their sister from them so long ago.

As Rulloff stood next to the dangling noose, Sheriff Martin spoke, "Mr. Rulloff it now lacks twenty-six minutes of the time fixed in my mind for carrying out the sentence of law. Have you anything to say to this audience?" Rulloff shook his head. The sheriff then asked if he wished to delay the matter. Rulloff again shook his head. A white hood was drawn over his head as he for the last time gazed out at the colors of life which surrounded him. The noose was then put around his neck and tightened. A strap was secured around his body to hold his arms in place, and his hands were placed in the back pockets of his pants. At thirty-five minutes past the hour, the weighted sack was released and Rulloff was pulled violently off the ground. His right hand was jerked out of his pocket as a result of the hanging. To the disbelief of the multitude of onlookers, Rulloff slowly placed his hand back into his pocket. This act caused quite a stir in the crowd, as reported by the *New York Times* the day after his death: "Eyes almost started from their sockets to see that hand move backward three or four inches and thrust itself into the pocket just as it was before. Human imagination would have never dared such a startling proof of the ruling passion strong in death."

After twenty minutes Rulloff was pronounced dead by Doctor Daniel S. Burr, and the body was lowered into an awaiting coffin. Although Rulloff had ordered Sheriff Martin to make sure his brother received his remains, other plans were in the works for what to do with his lifeless corpse. Rulloff's coffin was brought to the office of Dr. Burr, where the body was removed and a plaster cast, also called a death mask, was made of his face. A cast made from that death mask still survives to this day and can be seen at the History Center in Ithaca, New York. After the death mask was completed, Rulloff's head was removed from his body by severing the neck between the fifth and sixth vertebrae. After the confiscation of his head, his body was returned to the coffin and buried in a Binghamton cemetery.

Dr. Burr then proceeded to dissect Rulloff's head. Through careful observation, he found that his skull was larger than the average man's and that his brain, once removed from his skull, weighed 59 ounces. This weight exceeds that of the average human brain, which is about 50 ounces. One of the largest brain weights ever recorded was that of the French naturalist Cuvier, whose brain weighed 65 ounces.

After the dissection, Rulloff's brain was brought to Cornell University, where it was added to the brain collection of Dr. Burt Wilder. Dr. Wilder began collecting human brains to try to establish if there was a relationship between the size of a person's brain and their intelligence. Today most neuroscientists believe that overall brain weight is not an accurate way to determine a person's intelligence. Rulloff's brain is perfectly preserved and can be seen today on exhibit in the Psychology Department's Wilder Brain Collection at Cornell University.

The final resting place of Edward Rulloff is not exactly known; however, the night after his headless body was buried, his grave was dug up at least three times by medical students, as reported in the *New York Times*. "There has been a lively competition for the possession of Rulloff's head. Three different parties opened the grave at Binghamton on Friday night, with a view to disinter the part of the body which had never been buried. The prize was in the hands of a committee of doctors, who found it as difficult to reach his brain as other people had to get to his moral consciousness."

And so it was that Edward H. Rulloff's time on earth came to an end. Not surprisingly, his death was surrounded with just as much excitement as were the fifty-two years of his life. Rulloff's exploits were so original that he most assuredly occupies a unique place in not only the history of New York State, but of our nation as well. His criminal activities challenged the legal foundations of the time and helped to establish important precedents for the future. Rulloff's legal wrangling also aided him in avoiding two sentences of execution.

His life as a frustrated scholar is equally intriguing. Instead of seeking out a more traditional way to support his work in the study of language, Rulloff assumed the role of leader of a small crime syndicate, supporting himself solely by manipulating a pair of thugs to provide for his every need. He yearned for the life of a distinguished scholar and occasionally lived that life, but only by perpetrating unspeakable crimes, assuring his place in history as one of the most unusual characters to live during the nineteenth century.

For all of the great knowledge that Rulloff possessed and sought to obtain, his egocentric tendencies and lack of morality were the fatal flaws in his character that eventually led to his undoing. As evidenced by the answers he gave to the physicians sent to interview him on behalf of the governor, he perceived the world with a detached objective attitude. Sadly, this wayward genius applied a similar point of view to society as well, often treating his family, friends, and acquaintances with cold indifference. In the end, Edward H. Rulloff's criminal practices, lifelong quest for knowledge, and desire for acceptance by the intellectual world would come at a very high price to those around him and ultimately, himself.

ACKNOWLEDGEMENTS

This book could not have been written without the help of the dedicated scholars and professionals who contributed invaluably to the completion of this work. I would especially like to thank the History Center in Tompkins County; the Cornell University Library System; the Binghamton Public Library; Tompkins County Public Library; Carl A. Kroch Library Division of Rare and Manuscript Collections at Cornell University; Clarion County Historical Society; the Dryden Historical Society; and Lawrence Corbett, for all of their invaluable resources.

BIBLIOGRAPHY

Abbott's Practice Reports New Series, Vol. XI. New York: Diossy & Co., 1886.

Brooks, John G. "Rulloff Case Stirred Tompkins County." *Ithaca Journal*, June 23, 1945.

Budd, Louis J. *Mark Twain, Collected Tales Sketches, Speeches, & Essays 1852-1890*. New York: Literary Classics of the United States Inc., 1992.

Burr, G. *Medic-Legal Notes on the Case of Edward H. Rulloff*. New York: D. Appleton & Co., 1871.

"The Case of Rulloff in the Court of Appeals." *Ithaca Journal*, June 23, 1858.

Chemistry report on the remains of Mrs. W. Schutt. Dewitt Historical Society, March 23, 1859.

Crapsey, E. *The Man of Two Lives*. New York: Walden & Payne Printers, 1871.

Davis, A.J. *History of Clarion County Pennsylvania*. Syracuse, NY: D. Mason & Co., 1887.

Dorlands Illustrated Medical Dictionary: 27th Edition. Philadelphia: W.B. Saunders Co., 1988.

Dubeau, Sharon. *New Brunswick Loyalists, A Bicentennial Tribute*. Agincourt, Ontario: Theraton Press, 1983.

Editorial, *Ithaca Journal*, March 9, 1859.

Editorial, *Ithaca Journal*, March 16, 1859.

Editorial, *Ithaca Journal*, March 23, 1859.

"Edward H. Rulloff." *American Journal of Insanity*, April 1872.

"E.H. Rulloff." *New York Times*, May 17, 1871.

Endres, Gene. "Days of Future Past—Time Traveling Along the Erie Canal." *Ithaca Times*, June 1995.

"Escape of Rulloff!" *Ithaca Journal*, May 18, 1857.

Finch, Francis M. "His Side of the Story." Unpublished poem. Dewitt Historical Society.

Freeman, E.H. *The Veil of Secrecy Removed*. Binghamton, NY: Carl & Freeman Publishers, 1871.

Goodrich, G.B. *History of Dryden New York*. Dreyden, NY: Dryden Herald Steam Printing House, 1898.

Gray and Vanderpool. "Report to the Governor of New York." May 12, 1871.

Haas, R. *Biographical Sketch of W.H. Rulofson: Pioneer Photographer of California*. Education Extension, University of California, 1953.

Halliday, S.D. *Rulloff: The Great Criminal and Philologist: 2nd Edition*. Ithaca, NY: Dewitt Historical Society, 1906.

"Home Matters." *Ithaca Journal*, July 14, 1858.

Krum, A.A. "Regarding Rulloff." *Ithaca Journal*, April 12, 1901.

Krum, A.A. "The Rulloff History." *The Weekly Ithacan*, November 30, 1907.

Langhorne, S. "A Substitute for Rulloff." *New York Tribune*, May 3, 1871.

Leaflet. 1859. Dewitt Historical Society.

Legal brief of Francis M. Finch. 1859. Kroch Library Division of Rare and Manuscript Collections, Cornell University.

Letter from E.H. Rulloff. *Binghamton Democratic Leader*, January 20, 1871.

Letter from E.H. Rulloff to Francis M. Finch. April 9, 1859. Kroch Library Division of Rare and Manuscript Collections, Cornell University.

Letter from E.H. Rulloff to Francis M. Finch. June 6, 1859. Kroch Library Division of Rare and Manuscript Collections, Cornell University.

Letter from E.H. Rulloff to Francis M. Finch. November 3, 1859. Kroch Library Division of Rare and Manuscript Collections, Cornell University.

Letter from E.H. Rulloff to his attorneys. March 16, 1858. Kroch Library Division of Rare and Manuscript Collections, Cornell University.

Letter from W.C. Barber to E.H. Rulloff. June 20, 1859. Kroch Library Division of Rare and Manuscript Collections, Cornell University.

Life, Trial and Execution of Edward H. Rulloff. Philadelphia: Barclay & Co., 1873.

"The People v. Rulloff." *Reports of Decisions in Criminal Cases: Vol. III.* Albany, NY: William Gould Law Bookseller, 1858.

"Personal Interview with E. H. Rulloff, R. H. Mather." Reprinted in the *New York Times*, April 23, 1871.

The Phrenological Journal and Life Illustrated, Vol. LIII, No. 3. September 1871.

"Preparing to Take Rulloff's Case to the General Term." *New York Times*, January 23, 1871.

Professor R. H. Mathers' interview with Rulloff. *Springfield Republican*, April 1871.

"Put None But Americans on Guard!" *Ithaca Journal*, May 18, 1857.

"Report and Conclusions of Drs. Gray and Vanderpool." *New York Times*, May 13, 1871.

Reward poster for Edward H. Rulloff. Issued by Sheriff R. J. Ives, Tompkins County. Dewitt Historical Society, May 29, 1857.

Ruhlen, M. *The Origin of Language*. New York: John Wiley & Sons, 1994.

"Rulloff." *New York Times*, May 18, 1871.

"Rulloff: The Sentence of Law Executed Upon the Murderer." *New York Times*, May 19, 1871.

Rulloff trial juror questionnaire. August 20, 1856. Kroch Library Division of Rare and Manuscript Collections, Cornell University.

"The Rulloff Trial." *New York Times*, January 7, 1871.

"Rulloff's Brain." *New York Times*, May 24, 1871.

"Rulloff's Petition." *Binghamton Leader*, April 28, 1871.

"Scene of a Startlingly Dramatic Character in Court." *New York Times*, January 7, 1871.

Smith, E.A. *Allegheny—A Century of Education 1815–1915*. Meadville, PA: Allegheny College History Co., 1916.

Smith, J.S. *History of Jefferson College*. Pittsburgh: J.T. Shryock Printers, 1857.

"Some Notable Trials." *New York Times*, December 15, 1895.

"Suspected Murder." *Ithaca Journal*, September 3, 1845.

Swanberg, W.A. "The Case of the 59 Ounce Brain." *True Magazine*, May 1953.

Testimony of M. Ostrander. *Ithaca Journal*, May 1857.

Transactions & Proceedings, The American Philological Association, Vol. I. New York: S.W. Green Printers, 1870.

Wisbey, Herbert A., Jr. "The Life and Death of Edward H. Rulloff." *The Crooked Lake Review*, May 1993.

ABOUT THE AUTHOR

Stephen Butz has authored and published numerous books on the subjects of science, technology, and history. He received his Bachelor's and Master's degrees from Cornell University and has taught Earth and Environmental Science at both the college and secondary school level for over ten years. Steve lives along the New York-Vermont Border where he continues to work on his various writing projects.